**America's Middle Schools:
Practices and Progress**

A 25 Year Perspective

WITHDRAWN

WITHDRAWN

National Middle School Association is dedicated to improving the educational experiences of young adolescents by providing vision, knowledge, and resources to all who serve them in order to develop healthy, productive, and ethical citizens.

AMERICA'S MIDDLE SCHOOLS: PRACTICES AND PROGRESS

A 25 YEAR PERSPECTIVE

C. KENNETH MCEWIN

THOMAS S. DICKINSON

DORIS M. JENKINS

National Middle School Association
Columbus, Ohio

**National Middle School Association
2600 Corporate Exchange Drive, Suite 370
Columbus, Ohio 43231**

Copyright© 1996 by National Middle School Association.

ISBN 1-56090-102-0

McEwin, C. Kenneth.
        America's middle schools : practices and progress : a 25 year
perspective / C. Kenneth McEwin, Thomas S. Dickinson, Doris Jenkins.
            p.   cm.
        Includes bibliographical references (p.   ).
        ISBN 1-56090-102-0 (pbk.)
        1. Middle schools -- United States -- History. I. Dickinson. Thomas S.
II. Jenkins, Doris, date. III. Title.
LB1623.5.M34 1996
373.2 36--dc20   96-10806

To three people who have always counted

Jenelle P. McEwin
Deborah A. Butler
Kenneth D. Jenkins

ABOUT THE AUTHORS

C. Kenneth McEwin is Professor of Curriculum and Instruction at Appalachian State University, Boone, North Carolina. He is an author, consultant, past-president of National Middle School Association, and recipient of the John H. Lounsbury Distinguished Service Award.

Thomas S. Dickinson is Associate Professor of Curriculum, Instruction, and Media Technology, Indiana State University, Terre Haute. A former editor of *Middle School Journal*, he has written many articles and reports and has served the profession in a variety of leadership positions.

Doris M. Jenkins is Professor of Curriculum and Instruction and Associate Dean of the Reich College of Education at Appalachian State University, Boone, North Carolina. Active in middle school education for many years, she has authored numerous professional publications.

TABLE OF CONTENTS

FOREWORD

If we could first know where we are and whither we are tending, we could better judge what to do and how to do it.

— Abraham Lincoln

Add the phrase, "where we came from" and this statement by Lincoln would fit perfectly as a justification for and an introduction to this important research study. Knowing where we are now – the present – knowing where we came from – the past – and knowing what the trends are provide a solid basis for charting the course of middle level education as we approach the twenty-first century.

The 1990s will likely be something of a watershed period for middle level education. The euphoria that accompanied the early growth in the 70s and 80s has subsided somewhat. The harsh realities that surround making "second level" changes have become all too apparent. The pervasive holding power of institutionalized schooling is confronted daily. Yet zealousness still characterizes reform efforts at the middle level. Optimism abounds, but just where are we?

It is time to take stock, to contemplate the reality of our present status, to confirm progress where it exists, and to accept the lack of it where that is the case. Until now we simply lacked the data needed to do these things. We know of progress in this case or that case. We have had glowing reports from one school or another, but had no way of generalizing. Now this major study has provided the information we lacked. By far the most comprehensive study ever conducted on the state of middle level schooling, it paints a detailed picture of just where we are in this major educational movement. The extent of the random sample makes it possible to generalize for the total population. The data are also broken down by organizational pattern so that conclusions can be drawn, for example, regarding intramurals in 5-8 schools as compared to intramurals in 7-8 schools. To tap all the data available in this major report one needs to not only read carefully the text but also examine the more than fifty tables found in the appendices. Mining the data in these tables yields some fascinating gems.

The extent of the status data provided by this study is truly remarkable, but what makes the report unique and of even more value is its ability to provide perspective, to make comparisons with the status of middle schools in 1968 and in 1988. The instrument that was used to gather data included items from the two earlier studies as well as many new items.

Armed with the details provided by this study, educators can make more informed decisions about next steps. And as the data make clear, there are many – and large – next steps that need to be taken. Progress is evident, yet painfully slow. Considering the clarion call for school reform that has been heard on nearly every hand and the widely accepted validity of the middle school concept, educators need to use these data as a basis for launching new reform initiatives.

One final note – as we read these objectively stated statistics and figures and contemplate the significance of a particular percentage gain or the little variance between two numbers from different years, it is well to remember that behind these numbers are classroom teachers, principals, and other educators. The yeomen service of these individuals has made possible the success of middle level education, a story unparalleled in American education. While we might hope for greater gain, we must not fail to recognize the extraordinary commitment to young adolescents exhibited by thousands of today's educators. When another study is done in the year 2010 and the results are compared with the 1993 results, I predict gains will be recorded that reflect the vitality of middle level education and the work of these pioneer educators.

— John H. Lounsbury

Part I

INTRODUCTION

1.

BACKGROUND INFORMATION

The rich history of the emergence of the American middle school is well documented in the middle school knowledge base, and therefore will not be repeated in this publication. However, the authors are very much aware of the many contributions of early pioneers of the middle school movement, for example William M. Alexander, John H. Lounsbury, Gordon Vars, and Donald Eichhorn. In fact this major reorganization of middle level education is young enough that those who helped establish it continue to play active leadership roles. These leaders and their colleagues have served as advocates, role models, and mentors to many others who have assumed positions of leadership in the middle school movement, for example Paul S. George, J. Howard Johnston, Conrad F. Toepfer, and John H. Swaim.

Just as significantly, many thousands of teachers, principals, and other middle level professional personnel have taken courageous stands and worked diligently to establish developmentally responsive middle schools for the nation's young adolescents. Professional associations, especially the National Middle School Association, have also played crucial roles. The remarkable success of the middle school movement is due in large part to the contributions of these individuals and groups.

THE CURRENT STUDY

This study was undertaken for at least two major purposes. The first was to obtain a data base which would provide a partial record of the successes of the middle school movement over a period of 25 years. These data would be valuable in assessing progress made and in targeting areas that need more intensive efforts. A second major reason for the study was to document current practice in the nation's middle level schools. The movement needed fresh status data to see how much has been accomplished and to chart courses that would lead to dramatic improvement in the effectiveness of middle level schools.

The authors also wish to extend their deep gratitude to the principals and other professional personnel at the 1,798 middle level schools who took time from their busy schedules to respond to this comprehensive survey. We hope that the information this survey makes available will prove to be useful to them and their colleagues. We also want to express our thanks to the staff at National Middle School Association headquarters and the Colleges of Education at Appalachian State University, Boone, North Carolina and Indiana State University, Terra Haute, Indiana, for their continuing support and encouragement. As always, John Lounsbury, with his in-depth knowledge of middle level education and his excellent editing skills, has greatly improved the quality of this book. We are privileged to know him as a mentor and friend.

ORGANIZATION OF THE REPORT

To take full advantage of the extensive information contained in this publication, it is important to understand the report's organization. While the narrative contains most of the salient points and many tables and figures, there is a wealth of data in the tables found only in the appendices. By examining the lists of tables and figures on the following pages the reader will sense the extent of the information contained in this report. Tables in the appendices are often mentioned in the text and are distinguished by having both a letter and a number (example: Table B5).

Part I. Introduction, includes essential background information, listings of tables and figures, and descriptions of the methodology utilized in the 1993 study. Relationships of the 1968, 1988, and 1993 studies are discussed and other details regarding the sample and related matters are presented.

Part II. Middle Schools: A Twenty-Five Year Perspective, presents selected findings from Alexander's 1968 study, Alexander and McEwin's 1988 study, and the 1993 study reported here. It provides current data on 6-8 middle school programs and practices and a twenty-five-year comparison of trends from 1968 to 1993. Selected tables also report data from 5-8, 7-8, and 7-9 schools. Major findings from the total study are summarized with emphasis placed on trends and their appropriateness, or lack thereof, in efforts to makes schools for young adolescents developmentally responsive.

Part III. In Summary and In Perspective, first presents recommendations for future actions that will help those responsible for the education and welfare of young adolescents move forward in their efforts to establish and maintain developmentally responsive middle schools. These are followed by some reflections on the data and the authors' analyses. Additionally, a list of all the works cited throughout the book is found at the end of Part III.

Part IV. Appendices, includes 56 tables containing comprehensive information regarding programs and practices in grades 5-8, 6-8, 7-8, and 7-9 schools. By consulting *Part III* and the tables included in the *Appendices*, complete data are available for all the grade organizations that were a part of the study (112 tables and figures). A copy of the survey instrument is also included as Appendix H.

LIST OF TABLES

Table   Page

LIST OF FIGURES

2.
THE 1968, 1988, AND 1993 STUDIES

The first comprehensive national study of middle schools was conducted by William M. Alexander during the 1967-68 school year. (This study is referred to as the 1968 study throughout the report). Results of this historic study were published in *A Survey of Organizational Patterns of Reorganized Middle Schools* (1968). Data from the survey have also been reported in numerous other publications since that time, (e.g., *The Emergent Middle School,* Alexander, Williams, Compton, Hines, Prescott, & Kealy, 1969, and *Schools in the Middle: Status and Progress,* Alexander, & McEwin, 1989b). Data from the 1968 study have been used extensively in the present study as a benchmark to provide a twenty-five-year perspective on programs and practices in America's public middle schools.

The definition of middle schools for the 1968 Alexander study was "A school having at least three grades and not more than five grades, and including at least grades six and seven" (Alexander, 1968, p. 1). By design, this definition did not include grades 7-9 junior high schools because of the study's focus on new emerging middle schools. To avoid repeating this definition numerous times, it is referred to throughout the 1993 study as the Alexander definition. After determining that there were 1,101 schools meeting this definition, a 10% random stratified sample was selected. Of these 110 middle schools, 60% were grades 6-8 schools, 27% grades 5-8 schools, with the remainder of schools including grades 4-8, 5-7, 6-9, and 4-7. The return rate for the 1968 study was 83%.

THE 1988 STUDY

Twenty years after the 1968 study, Alexander and McEwin conducted a comprehensive follow-up study of America's public middle level schools during the 1987-88 school year (Alexander & McEwin, 1989b).

(This study is referred to as the 1988 study throughout this report). Several additional studies conducted in the intervening years between 1968 and 1988 replicated, at least in part, many of the items of the 1968 study. These and related studies may be of interest to the reader (Compton, 1976; Brooks & Edwards, 1978). Additional relevant studies that provide important related data on middle level programs and practices in the twenty-five years between 1968 and 1993 are used in the present study (McEwin & Clay, 1983; Cawelti, 1988; Epstein & Mac Iver, 1990; Valentine, Clark, Irvin, Keefe, & Melton, 1993). These studies, in combination with this publication, offer the reader a comprehensive understanding of the changing nature of middle schools during the past two and a half decades.

Many survey items from the 1968 Alexander study of middle level schools were replicated in the 1988 Alexander and McEwin study. However, some new items were added to provide a more complete picture of programs and practices present. An additional difference in the two studies was that the 1988 study included grades 5-8, 7-8 and 7-9 schools as well as 6-8 schools. This did not negatively affect the comparison with earlier middle school practices since the data were separated by grade organization during analysis. Results from the 1988 study are reported in two separate publications. The research report, *Earmarks of Schools in the Middle: A Research Report* (Alexander & McEwin, 1989a), presents the data organized by individual grade organizations. The second publication, *Schools in the Middle: Status and Progress* (Alexander & McEwin, 1989), includes much of the same data as the research report. However, in this 1989 monograph, the researchers combined results from grades 5-8 and 6-8 schools because of the small amount of variance in the data and because of the popularity of middle schools with these grade configurations. Since the 1993 study did find some rather significant differences in programs and practices in these grade organizations, results from 5-8 and 6-8 schools are reported separately.

THE 1993 STUDY

The data for this study were gathered during the 1992-93 school year. (This study is referred to as the 1993 study throughout the report). Separately organized middle schools with grade organizations 5-8, 6-8, 7-8, and 7-9 were selected since the large majority of America's young adolescents attend schools with these grade organizations. For example, approximately 80% of all seventh graders attend schools with one of these grade organizations as compared to only 9% who attend grades K-8 schools (Epstein & Mac Iver, 1990, p. 5).

A national, random, stratified 30% sample of schools containing grades 5-8, 6-8, 7-8, and 7-9 was drawn. The 30% random sample was selected from each grade organization so that results would be representative of those respective grade organizations (Table 1). For example, since there were 6,155 grades 6-8 schools, 30% of those schools (1,846) were mailed survey forms. In comparison, there were only 1,425 grades 7-9 schools which meant that surveys were mailed to 428 schools with that grade organization. This sample selection procedure helped guarantee a more accurate reflection of programs and practices. Data in the current study were analyzed in ways that provide a 25 year historical perspective of 6-8 middle schools, and present comprehensive data on programs and practices in all grade organizations included in the study.

Table 1 contains information about the number of schools with the selected grade organizations at the time of the study, the number of surveys mailed to the 30% sample of those schools, and the number and percentages of returns for each organization and the total study. Percentages of the total study made up of responding schools with each grade organization are also presented.

TABLE 1
POPULATION, SAMPLE, AND RESPONSES

Grade Organization	Number of Schools	Number of Surveys Mailed	Number of Surveys Returned	Percent Returned	Percent of Total Study
Grades 5-8	1,223	367	195	53	11
Grades 6-8	6,155	1,846	1,031	56	57
Grades 7-8	2,412	724	406	56	23
Grades 7-9	1,425	428	166	39	9
Total Study	11,215	3,365	1,798	53	100

One thousand seven hundred and ninety-eight (1,798) schools that were mailed surveys responded for an overall return rate of 53%. Surveys were received from all 50 states and the District of Columbia. Table 2 presents a state-by-state breakdown of the number of responses received from each state. The highest percentages of returns were from grades 6-8 and 7-8 schools (56%), with grades 5-8 schools achieving a return rate of 53%. The return rate for grades 7-9 schools was 39%, a percentage lower than the other three grade organizations, but high enough to en-sure the reliability and validity of the data from those schools (Table 1). The percentages of schools with each grade organization mirrored con-figurations which comprised the total sample, and therefore the grade organizations of middle level schools in the United States. For example, 55% of grades 6-8 schools were mailed surveys and 54% of surveys returned for the total study were from those schools. Similarly, 13% of grades 7-9 schools were sent surveys and 9% of the total returns were from schools with that grade organization. □

TABLE 2
NUMBER OF RESPONSES BY STATE

STATE	NUMBER	STATE	NUMBER
Alabama	23	Nevada	11
Alaska	3	New Hampshire	14
Arizona	26	New Jersey	54
Arkansas	11	New Mexico	7
California	143	New York	88
Colorado	27	North Carolina	59
Connecticut	25	North Dakota	4
Delaware	4	Ohio	74
Florida	61	Oklahoma	21
Georgia	52	Oregon	35
Hawaii	4	Pennsylvania	70
Idaho	14	Rhode Island	6
Illinois	82	South Carolina	31
Indiana	46	South Dakota	10
Iowa	44	Tennessee	27
Kansas	31	Texas	141
Kentucky	25	Utah	17
Louisiana	23	Vermont	2
Maine	15	Virginia	46
Maryland	25	Washington	48
Massachusetts	43	West Virginia	14
Michigan	86	Wisconsin	42
Minnesota	30	Wyoming	13
Mississippi	15	Other (D.C.)	1
Missouri	40	State Not Identified	38
Montana	13		
Nebraska	14	Total	1798

Part II

MIDDLE SCHOOLS: A 25 YEAR PERSPECTIVE

3.

Enrollments, Articulation, and Dates of Establishment

Although school size is a popular topic of discussion and debate, there is no research base which establishes the optimum size of schools. Some studies have asked middle level school principals what school size they consider to be ideal. For example, 41% of respondents in a 1992 national survey considered the optimum middle level school to be between 400 and 599 students. The second most frequently selected school size was 600 to 799 students (Valentine, et al., 1993).

Some parents, educators, and others believe that small schools are automatically better than medium size or large schools. Others assume that larger schools are superior because they offer a greater variety of classes, programs, and instructional grouping options than smaller schools. However, school size tends to vary with population shifts and other factors largely unrelated to decisions about the best school size for young adolescents. The overall quality of middle level schools continues to be more closely related to factors such as the quality of programs, teachers, leadership, organizational plans, and grouping practices.

Sizes of enrollments in the sample ranged from less than 100 to more than 2000. Enrollment sizes were placed into the categories of 1-400, 401-800, and more than 800, for each of the three studies. As shown in Table 3, middle schools with enrollments of 401-800 have remained the most popular size throughout the 25 years considered in this study. The percentages of small schools (1-400) did not change significantly from 1968 (39%) to 1988 (34%), but a notable decrease occurred in the five-year time span from 1988 to 1993 (34% to 22%). During these same time periods, the percentages of large schools with enrollments more than 800, after increasing only 2% in 20 years, increased from 14% in 1988 to 30% in 1993. These changes indicate that while a significant number of middle schools had enrollments in the 401-800 range (48%)

in 1993, percentages of schools with small enrollments (1-400) had decreased while middle schools with larger enrollments (more than 800) increased rather dramatically in five years.

TABLE 3
GRADES 6-8 MIDDLE SCHOOL ENROLLMENTS
1968, 1988, & 1993

Range of Enrollment	Percent		
	1968	1988	1993
1-400	39	34	22
401-800	45	52	48
Over 800	16	14	30

In 1993 the most common enrollment percentages in 5-8 and 7-8 schools were the 401-800 category (Table 4). However, the highest percentage of enrollment in grades 7-9 schools was 800 or more (57%). Clearly, 7-9 schools were found to have larger student populations than the other grade organizations included in this study. Only 6% of grades 7-9 junior high schools enrolled 400 or fewer students. When the total study was considered, 22% of all middle level schools had enrollments of 400 or fewer, 48% had enrollments of 401-800, and 30% enrolled 800 or more (Table 4).

TABLE 4
ENROLLMENTS BY GRADE ORGANIZATION

Range of Enrollment	Percent				
	5-8	6-8	7-8	7-9	All
1-400	29	22	25	6	22
401-800	58	48	50	37	48
Over 800	13	30	25	57	30

The trend toward larger middle schools raises concerns among those who question the ability of these larger schools to be developmentally responsive to the needs of young adolescents. It should be noted, however, that school size is probably not the major determinant of successful middle schools. There are highly effective schools of all enrollment sizes. It is much more likely that decisions regarding the successful implementation of responsive programs determine the ultimate success of programs (Epstein & Mac Iver, 1990).

ARTICULATION

One of the six original functions of the junior high school, and its modern successor the middle school, was that of articulation – bridging the educational transition from childhood to adolescence for its clients. Gruhn and Douglass, respected authorities on junior high school education, noted in 1947 that one of the functions of the junior high school was: "To provide a gradual transition from pre-adolescent education to an educational program suited to the needs and interests of adolescent boys and girls" (p. 60). Today this function remains a vital part of the mission and operation of middle schools and has been expanded to include the transition from middle school to the high school. Because of increasing concerns for making K-12 schooling a continuous system of movement for students with the least possible disruption, and yet still provide appropriate educational opportunities and programs, the dual bridging function played by middle schools is becoming even more important (Carnegie Council on Adolescent Development, 1989).

Middle schools have, since their inception, employed multiple means of articulating with elementary and high schools. This is particularly true relative to the actual physical transition between very different school organizations, curriculums, and programs. For many young adolescents the transition from the elementary school to the middle school means a major change in the number of peers and adults they interact with daily; how the curriculum is conceptualized, organized, and delivered; and the programs available to students. The use of multiple simultaneous paths of articulation on the part of middle schools is an effort to insure that multiple target audiences – teachers, parents, and students – as well as curriculum and programs will be impacted.

Data collected in the 1993 survey, as well as data reported from the studies in 1968 and 1988, reported in Table 5, indicate positive and continuing trends as well as noteworthy accomplishments in the area of articulation for 6-8 schools. (Table A1 reports the 1993 results of means of articulation for all grade organizations and for the total study).

In the 1993 study, the most prominent articulation practice that 6-8 schools employed was visitations by elementary students from feeder schools. Visits to middle schools were used by 90% of the 6-8 schools. The second most prominent articulation practice was obtaining or providing student data on entering or exiting students (84%). This category has shown a small increase since 1988 after decreasing from 90% in 1968 to 78% in 1988. The trend seems to be moving back toward the previous 1968 high of 90% (Table 5). Providing information to feeder and receiving schools was the third most employed articulation activity

TABLE 5
MEANS OF ARTICULATION
1968, 1988, & 1993

Means of Articulation	Percent		
	1968	1988	1993
Joint Workshops With Teachers in Lower and/or Higher Grades	67	70	65
Joint Curriculum Planning Activities With Teachers of Lower and/or Higher Grades	74	66	64
Middle School Teacher Visitation of Elementary and/or High School	40	40	44
Giving Program Information to Elementary and/or High School	62	76	80
Obtaining or Providing Data Regarding the Students Leaving or Entering Your School	90	78	84
Student Visitation of the High School(s) for Orientation	54	73	78
Visitation of Your School by Students from Feeder Schools	52	86	90
Middle School Student Visits to Feeder Schools to Acquaint Elementary Students With Your Programs and Activities	15	38	51
Visitation of Your School by High School Representatives for the Purpose of Orientation	57	72	77

1968: Alexander definition
1988: Grades 6-8 middle schools
1993: Grades 6-8 middle schools

(80%). Student orientation visits to the high school were used by 78% of 6-8 schools while 77% hosted visits by high school personnel.

Seven of nine activities in the 1993 study show either modest or significant increases across the 25 year period (Table 5). The two activities that showed small declines may be activities that do not have the same degree of relevance for middle level schools in the 1990s as they did 25 years ago (Joint curriculum planning showed a small but continuing decline). The small decline in joint workshops with teachers in lower and/or higher grades and the small and continuing decline in joint curriculum planning activities with teachers of lower and/or higher grades may not be as critical a decline because of the establishment and viability of the middle school as an equal partner with elementary and high schools and the establishment of a strong middle school curriculum with particular unique elements (interdisciplinary and an exploration focus) between the broad general elementary curriculum and the more narrowly-focused separate subject curriculum of high schools.

Using middle school students as a part of program orientation teams for visits to feeder schools is now practiced by a majority of 6-8 schools in this survey (51%). While this activity has increased significantly from extremely modest beginnings in 1968 (15%), it seems to hold significant promise as an agent of positive change, not only for elementary students who can engage with peers about their transition, but also for the middle school student involved in such programs.

Figure 1 provides information concerning articulation issues through illustrating the significant increase in selected articulation activities over the 25 year period from 1968 to 1993. Five articulation activities that showed continuous growth, and ones that the majority of 6-8 schools in this study engaged in, are portrayed. The five most prevalent activities that the vast majority of middle schools engaged in (77% or higher) are visitations of middle schools by students from feeder elementary schools (90%), sharing student data on entering or exiting students (84%), providing program information to sending and receiving schools (80%), student visitations of high schools for orientation (78%), and visitations by high school representatives for program information (77%).

While the most prevalent activities mentioned above are significant, it is also significant that while visitations are occurring by students from the elementary and the middle school (90% and 78% respectively), a minority of schools used visitations of the elementary feeder schools and/or the high school receiver schools by middle level teachers (44%)

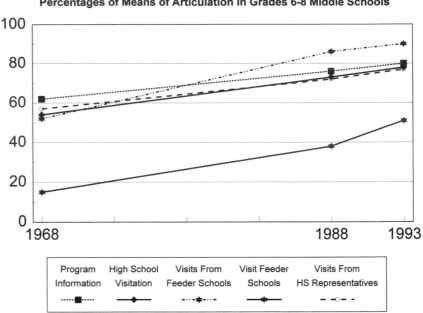

Figure 1
Percentages of Means of Articulation in Grades 6-8 Middle Schools

	Program Information	High School Visitation	Visits From Feeder Schools	Visit Feeder Schools	Visits From HS Representatives
	·····■·····	——◆——	-···★···-	——★——	- -○- -

(Table 5). The typical tendency of teachers, at any level, is to stay close to home. The authors hope, however, that middle school teachers themselves, will increase the effectiveness of articulation with their sister schools through formal visitationss to learn more about the sending and receiving schools, their programs and practices, and use these activities to form stronger linkage for their common students. This increase in visitations would further enhance articulation and the effect that all school organizations have on students.

ESTABLISHING 6-8 MIDDLE SCHOOLS

In 1963 William M. Alexander called for a new school in the middle in his now historic speech in Ithaca, New York, at the Cornell University Junior High School Conference (Alexander, 1995). Since that time separately organized 6-8 middle schools have been established throughout the United States while the middle school's predecessor, the 7-9 junior high school, has declined dramatically.

Results from the 1993 study indicate a strong continuing trend of establishing 6-8 middle schools within this country. As the data in Table 6 indicate, 29% of the 6-8 schools in this 1993 study were established in the period 1988-92 and 59% established after 1980. As well, the trend of establishing 6-8 middle schools for young adolescents holds for the twenty-year time period of 1972-1992. In contrast, 75% of 7-9 junior high schools in the study were established prior to 1980 (Table A2).

TABLE 6
DATES OF ESTABLISHMENT OF GRADES 6-8 SCHOOLS
1988 & 1993

Year of Study	Percent					
	Before 1955	1955-62	1963-71	1972-79	1980-87	1988-92
1988	2	3	25	35	35	--
1993	4	4	12	21	30	29

Table A2, which provides the data for all middle level school organizations in the study (grades 5-8, 6-8, 7-8, and 7-9), supports this continuing trend for establishing schools organized as 5-8 and 7-8 middle schools with 16% and 24% increases, respectively, for the 1988-1992 period. The twenty-year trend for these two organizational entities is significant and comparable in its continued growth to that of the 6-8 school (5-8 schools, 1972-1992, 76% increase; 7-8 schools, 1972-1992, 61% increase).

PREPARATION PRIOR TO OPENING A MIDDLE SCHOOL

Establishing a middle school is an important decision for an educational community. It is understandable that many different individuals and groups would be involved in this effort and that it would most often be preceded by a variety of activities by a district and the staff members involved with the new 6-8 middle school (Table 7). Planning for a new middle school may be one of the most important investments to yield appropriate education for young adolescents, especially with the continuing small numbers of middle school teachers with specialized preparation (Figure 17). Therefore it is not surprising that all preparatory activities show continued growth across the 1968-1993 period (Table 7). It should be noted that many 6-8 schools engage in a variety of the activities indicated in Table 7, and it is conceivable that the preparations for a new 6-8 middle school would involve multiple activities that build and expand to the actual school opening.

TABLE 7
MIDDLE SCHOOLS USING CERTAIN PREPARATORY
ACTIVITIES PRIOR TO ORIGINAL OPENING
1968, 1988, & 1993

Activity	Percent		
	1968	1988	1993
Year or More Faculty Study and District Planning	25	53	54
Year or More Study by Faculty Representatives at College or University	2	6	8
Representation in Specially Funded Planning Project	2	16	23
Summer Faculty Workshop Prior to School Opening	5	27	40
Occasional Planning Sessions of Prospective School Faculty Members	52	63	71
Visitation of School With Similar Plans Operating	38	72	78
Inservice Meetings of Prospective Faculty Members With Consultants	26	58	67

1968: Alexander definition
1988: Grades 6-8 schools
1993: Grades 6-8 schools

A new middle school cannot just be willed into excellence. Knowledgeable educators who believe in the appropriate education of young adolescents know that planning a new middle school is a challenging activity. Therefore, it is not surprising that the majority of 6-8 middle schools in the study (54%) used a year or more of faculty study and district planning prior to the original opening of the school. This majority continues the trend of a year or more preparation that was first indicated in 1968.

While a year or more of faculty study and district planning is a significant investment in preparation for a new middle school, there are other important activities, albeit less time-intensive, that are engaged in by a significant number of 6-8 schools. The most often cited preparatory activity was the visitation of another middle school with similar operating plans (78%). This was followed by occasional planning sessions of prospective school faculty members (71%), inservice meetings of prospective school faculty members with consultants (67%), the previously mentioned year of study and planning (54%) and summer faculty workshops prior to school opening (40%). The data indicate that representation in specially funded planning projects, while still small (23%), continues to grow – from 2% in 1968, to 16% in 1988, and 23% in 1993.

GRADE ORGANIZATION DECISIONS

Table A3 provides the data for the total study on the persons (or groups) determining grade organization for those schools established after 1987. While the individuals and groups making these decisions continue to be system level administrators and principals (91% for system-wide administrators and 69% for principals), as was the case with the 1968 and 1988 studies (system-wide administrators, 1968, 78%; 1988, 88%; building principals, 1968, 69%; 1988, 71%), teachers' involvement in grade organization decisions continues to show modest gains overall with 54% involved in this decision in 1993, up from 46% in 1968, and 50% in 1988. It is interesting to note that overall the greatest involvement by teachers in grade organization decisions is by teachers in 5-8 and 7-8 schools respectively (Table A3).

In all the school organization types in the total study, parents were involved in the grade organization decision 38% of the time. This continues the relatively low level of parent involvement in grade organization decisions. □

4.

MIDDLE SCHOOL INSTRUCTIONAL ORGANIZATION

Most supporters of the middle school concept also now subscribe to certain common elements believed to be congruent with the goals of educating students in virtually all middle level schools. Advisory programs, interdisciplinary team organization, an exploratory emphasis on the curriculum combined with a core of common knowledge, flexible scheduling, active instruction, specially trained teachers, shared decision-making among the professionals in the school, success experiences for all students, improved health and physical education, and reconnecting the home and community with the education of young adolescent learners; this is the canon of contemporary middle school education. National, state, and local organizations and associations affirm it (New York State Department of Education, 1989; Carnegie, 1989). The national debate about the common characteristics of middle level schools is over (George, 1991, p. 2).

Given an accepted canon of middle school education, how are today's middle schools organized to provide appropriate programs and practices for young adolescents? The 1993 survey instrument included several sections designed to help determine trends in the use of particular organizational structures in grades 6-8 middle schools. Specifically, this chapter examines six major school organization structures:

1. Core subject area organizational plans
2. Team leader selection
3. The organizational plans for health and reading
4. Teacher planning periods
5. Remedial arrangements
6. Scheduling plans

CORE SUBJECT AREA ORGANIZATIONAL PLANS

Since 1968 there has been a steady increase in the use of interdisciplinary teams as an organizational plan for 6-8 middle schools in the four core subject areas of language arts, mathematics, science, and social studies at all grade levels (Tables 8, 9, 10 & 11). From very modest beginnings of 5% to 8% of the four core areas organized as interdisciplinary teams in 1968 to current widespread usage, the 1993 study shows interdisciplinary teams at the three grade levels in 6-8 middle schools to be growing toward the predominant instructional plan for core area instruction. As well, during the period 1968-1993, significant declines in departmentalization at the sixth, seventh, and eighth grade levels have occurred, this directly coupled with the rise in the use of interdisciplinary teams.

LANGUAGE ARTS

Table 8 provides data on language arts organizational plans in 6-8 middle schools for all three studies. As with other subject areas included in the core (mathematics, science and social studies), since 1968 there has been a steady increase in the use of interdisciplinary teams as an organizational plan for language arts instruction. In Alexander's original survey in 1968 language arts classrooms were part of interdisciplinary team organizations in 8% of the schools at the sixth grade, and in 6% at the seventh and eighth grade levels. This figure has increased over the last twenty-five years to over half of the 6-8 middle schools in this study using interdisciplinary teams at the sixth (59%) and seventh grade levels (53%). While the eighth grade level in language arts is still organized as departments in half of the schools in the study (50%), this too has seen a significant decline (Table 8). Figure 2 provides a graphical representation of the data for language arts classrooms for 6-8 middle schools in all three surveys over the 25-year period of 1968 to 1993.

The most significant increase in the use of interdisciplinary team organization in language arts classrooms between the 1988 and 1993 studies occurred at the sixth grade level (33%, 1988; 59%, 1993). During the period 1968 to 1993, self-contained classrooms at the sixth grade level declined from 30% to 11% (Table 8). The use of the interdisciplinary team organization is now recognized as appropriate for the youngest client in the 6-8 middle school, the young adolescent in the sixth grade.

TABLE 8
LANGUAGE ARTS ORGANIZATIONAL PLANS
1968, 1988, & 1993

Subject Area	Grade	Percent								
		Interdisciplinary Team			Departmentalization			Self-Contained		
		'68	'88	'93	'68	'88	'93	'68	'88	'93
Language Arts	6	8	33	59	35	44	29	30	18	11
	7	6	40	53	74	66	43	1	6	5
	8	6	31	45	74	71	50	1	6	5

1968: Alexander definition
1988: Grades 6-8 schools
1993: Grades 6-8 schools

Figure 2
Percentages of Language Arts Organizational Plans
Grades 6-8 Schools -- Grade Six

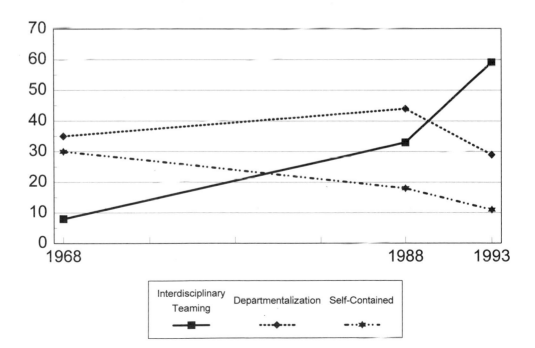

As noted earlier, the use of departmentalization has experienced significant declines over the course of the three studies. The data from the 1968 study show that departmentalization was used in 74% of the eighth grade classrooms sampled, yet by 1993, this usage had dropped to 50%, with the most significant decrease coming in the years between 1988 and 1993 (71%, 1988; 50%, 1993). Similar findings regarding departmentalization in seventh grade language arts classrooms were found in 6-8 schools (74%, 1968; 66%, 1988; 43%, 1993).

MATHEMATICS

Mathematics classrooms follow the organizational discussion above concerning interdisciplinary team organization in 6-8 middle schools. The 1993 study shows significant increases in the use of interdisciplinary team organization for all three grade levels across all three studies (Table 9). The sixth grade has moved from 8% of the schools in the 1968 study using interdisciplinary team organization for mathematics to 37% in 1988 and 58% in 1993. Similar increases are reported for the seventh (6%, 1968; 27%, 1988; 49%, 1993) and the eighth grade (6%, 1968; 23%, 1988; 42%, 1993).

TABLE 9
MATHEMATICS ORGANIZATIONAL PLANS
1968, 1988, & 1993

Subject Area	Grade	Percent								
		Interdisciplinary Team			Departmentalization			Self-Contained		
		'68	'88	'93	'68	'88	'93	'68	'88	'93
Math	6	8	37	58	50	48	32	24	16	11
	7	6	27	49	88	71	46	0	5	5
	8	6	23	42	89	75	53	0	4	5

1968: Alexander definition
1988: Grades 6-8 schools
1993: Grades 6-8 schools

Mathematics classrooms reflect the twenty-five-year trend, as do their counterparts in language arts classrooms, of the parallel increase/decline between interdisciplinary team organization and departmentalization. In 1968 half of the sixth grade mathematics classrooms in 6-8 middle schools were departmentalized. Seventh and eighth grade classrooms were overwhelmingly using departmental organization in 1968 (seventh, 88%; eighth, 89%). Over the twenty years between Alexander's original 1968 study and the 1988 study the organization of mathematics classrooms in 6-8 middle schools began to be transformed. The 1988 study reported declines in the use of departmentalization at all three grade levels (Table 9). This trend is most visible in the current study of 6-8 middle schools. Less than half of the schools in the current study use departmental organization in sixth (32%) and seventh (46%) grades. Only at the eighth grade level is departmentalization used in the majority (53%) of the schools for mathematics classrooms, and this grade level use of departmentalization showed a decline between the 1988 and 1993 studies of 75% to 53% (Table 9). As well, the use of self-contained classrooms for mathematics instruction at the sixth grade level continues to decline (down from 24% in 1968 to 16% in 1988, and 11% in 1993).

SCIENCE

Figure 3 illustrates graphically the trend of increasing usage of interdisciplinary team organization and declining usage of departmentalization by portraying the three major organizational plans in eighth grade science in 6-8 grade middle schools. Science organizational plans, are, like their counterparts in language arts and mathematics, moving toward interdisciplinary team organization as the dominant instructional organization plan in 6-8 middle schools (Table 10).

As the 1993 study shows, interdisciplinary team organization was used by more than half (58%) of the sixth grades in the sample. Seventh and eighth grades are approaching this point with 49% of seventh grade and 44% of the eighth grade classrooms organized in this manner. Again, as in the case of language arts and mathematics, there were significant increases at all three grade levels between 1988 and 1992. At the sixth grade level the increase between 1988 and 1992 was from 36% to 58%; seventh grade from 26% to 49%; and eighth grade from 22% to 44%.

The decline in departmentalization in science continues from its dominant position in 1968 (50% of the sixth grade science classrooms and

87% of the seventh and eighth grade classrooms) to 1993 levels where only at the eighth grade is departmentalization used in over half of the classrooms for science. Significant declines in the use of self-contained classrooms at the sixth grade level are also reported in Table 10.

Figure 3
Percentages of Science Organizational Plans
Grades 6-8 Schools -- Grade Eight

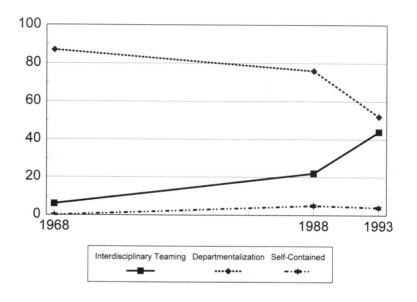

Interdisciplinary Teaming   Departmentalization   Self-Contained

TABLE 10
SCIENCE ORGANIZATIONAL PLANS
1968, 1988, & 1993

Subject Area	Grade	Percent								
		Interdisciplinary Team			Departmentalization			Self-Contained		
		'68	'88	'93	'68	'88	'93	'68	'88	'93
Science	6	7	36	58	50	47	32	26	16	10
	7	5	26	49	87	71	46	0	4	4
	8	6	22	44	87	76	52	0	5	4

1968:   Alexander definition
1988:   Grades 6-8 schools
1993:   Grades 6-8 schools

SOCIAL STUDIES

The final core subject area, social studies, shows similar trends in the use of organizational plans – a significant rise in interdisciplinary team organization and significant declines in departmentalization and self-contained classrooms. As with the other core areas of language arts, mathematics, and science, social studies has shown an increase in the use of interdisciplinary team organization at all three grade levels of 6-8 middle schools across all three studies (Table 11). During the period between the original Alexander 1968 study and the current study, inter-disciplinary team organization usage for social studies by the schools in this study increased 52% at the sixth grade level, 53% at the seventh grade level, and 39% at the eighth grade level. Currently, over half of the 6-8 middle schools in this study are using interdisciplinary team organization for social studies at the sixth and seventh grade levels (59% and 58%, respectively) while 45% are employing this plan at the eighth grade level (Table 11).

Fifty-one percent of eighth grade classrooms in the study utilized de-partmentalization, down from 72% in the 1988 study. Current usage at the sixth and seventh grade levels (31% and 38%, respectively) de-clined from previous studies. Self-contained classroom organization declined for social studies organization at the sixth grade level – from a high of 32% in 1968, to 17% in 1988, and 11% in 1993 (Table 11).

TABLE 11
SOCIAL STUDIES ORGANIZATIONAL PLANS
1968, 1988, & 1993

Subject Area	Grade	Percent								
		Interdisciplinary Team			Departmentalization			Self-Contained		
		'68	'88	'93	'68	'88	'93	'68	'88	'93
Social Studies	6	7	37	59	39	46	31	32	17	11
	7	5	28	58	80	68	38	1	4	4
	8	6	23	45	76	72	51	2	5	4

1968: Alexander definition
1988: Grades 6-8 schools.
1993: Grades 6-8 schools.

The use of interdisciplinary team organization, particularly those teams that are organized around the core subject areas of language arts, mathematics, science, and social studies, is a dominant trend in 6-8 middle schools. The data reported here from the current and previous studies clearly illustrate the decline of departmentalization and the rise in team organization. This decline in departmentalization and increase in interdisciplinary team organization was also confirmed in a 1992 national study of middle level schools (Valentine, et al., 1993). When results from these two recent national studies – Valentine, et al., 1993 and the current study – are compared with earlier national studies, it is apparent that the use of interdisciplinary team organization in middle schools has increased substantially, and has in fact become the norm rather than the exception in middle schools (Educational Research Service, 1969; Mellinger & Rackauskas, 1970; Brooks & Edwards, 1978; Valentine, Clark, Nickerson, & Keefe, 1981; McEwin & Clay, 1983; Cawelti, 1988; & Epstein & Mac Iver, 1990).

What is most significant about this trend is what the authors of the current study believe to be the underlying conviction that has taken hold: the recognition by growing numbers of middle level educators that departmentalization simply is not an appropriate way to organize instruction for this age group while the interdisciplinary team organization is most appropriate. Team organization is truly, from our perspective as well as that of others (George, 1991), part of the canon of the modern middle school.

TEAM LEADER SELECTION

If 6-8 middle schools are governed by a new organizational paradigm, then how is this new paradigm governed? How are interdisciplinary team organizations governed and led? The 1993 study attempted to answer this question by examining how middle level schools selected team leaders. Table 12 reports the results of this inquiry for the various middle level school organizations (grades 5-8, 6-8, 7-8, and 7-9) and the total study; while Figure 4 graphically presents data regarding team leader selection for the total study.

While the method of team leader selection in the four different grade organization structures of middle level schools in the study are relatively stable across those organizations, a number of findings emerge (Table 12):

1. 5-8 schools were most likely to have no team leaders (28%);
2. 5-8 schools compared to the other grade organizations were less likely to have a team leader elected by team members (16%);
3. Team leaders in 5-8 schools were more likely to be appointed by the principal (20%) than in other organizations;
4. The dominant mode for team leader selection in 6-8 schools was evenly split between principal-appointed and team-elected team leaders (26%); and,
5. 7-8 and 7-9 schools were slightly more likely to have team leaders elected than any other grade organization (29%).

When the total study is examined (Figure 4), priorities for the four grade organizations emerge. The most popular means of selecting team leaders was election by team members (26%), followed by principal appointment (24%). No team leader was present in 20% of the teams, while 16% of the teams rotated leadership responsibility. In 11% of the teams in the total study the leader emerges informally, rather than through election, appointment, or rotation. A similar pattern was found in a 1992 national study (Valentine, et al., 1993).

It is accurate to say that at this point in the development of the middle level school, no one dominant means for selecting team leaders has emerged (Table 12). Additional investigation is called for in at least three areas:

1. For the 20% of the schools in the total study that responded with "no team leader," the question remains: How does this affect their operation?
2. For the 11% of the schools in the total study that responded with "leader emerges informally," there are the questions: Is this an ongoing emergence? and, Once a leader emerges, does he/she continue?
3. Finally, which form(s) of leadership selection are most successful for interdisciplinary team organizations?

This study, planned to be a wide snapshot of middle schools in America over a broad range of concerns, did not attempt to approach the question of effectiveness. This is particularly true of the effectiveness of any or all of the methods of selecting team leaders discussed above.

TABLE 12
TEAM LEADER SELECTION

Method for Selecting Team Leaders	Percent				
	5-8	6-8	7-8	7-9	All
No Team Leader	28	18	23	16	20
Appointed by Principal	20	26	18	25	24
Elected by Team Members	16	26	29	29	26
Leader Rotates From Among Team	18	15	16	13	16
Leader Emerges Informally	13	11	11	14	11
Other	6	3	3	3	3

Figure 4
Team Leader Selection -- Total Study

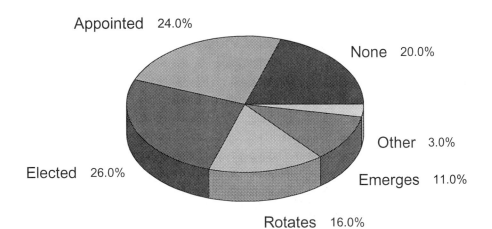

Appointed   24.0%

None   20.0%

Other   3.0%

Elected   26.0%

Emerges   11.0%

Rotates   16.0%

HEALTH AND READING

The 1993 study examined instructional organization plans in two critical areas of young adolescent schooling outside the four core subject areas of language arts, mathematics, science, and social studies. Health education and reading, two instructional areas that relate to long-term academic and personal healthy development for young adolescents, were examined to determine trends in organization patterns.

HEALTH EDUCATION

Health education and its connection to the healthy development of young adolescents is a recognized fact (Carnegie Council on Adolescent Development, 1989). This is particularly true with the increasing focus on risk factors and risk behaviors that involve young adolescents (Dryfoos, 1990; Hechinger, 1992; National Commission on the Role of the School and the Community in Improving Adolescent Health, 1990). The current study examined ways health education was organized in 6-8 middle schools by examining the use of three primary instructional organizational plans for delivering health education to young adolescents:

1. as a separate subject;
2. in conjunction with physical education; or
3. in conjunction with science.

Table 13 illustrates the use of these three primary organizational plans for 6-8 middle schools in the current study.

TABLE 13
ORGANIZATIONAL PLANS FOR HEALTH
GRADES 6-8 SCHOOLS

Instructional Plans	Percent		
	Grade 6	Grade 7	Grade 8
Separate Subject	37	42	42
With P. E.	13	14	17
With Science	42	38	35
Other	7	6	6

The two most prevalent patterns for delivering health education in 6-8 middle schools vary with grade level, although both patterns are relatively equal in their use by those schools in the current study (Table 13). For sixth graders, the most popular pattern is for health to be incorporated with science (42%). Health taught as a separate subject occupies the second most prevalent pattern (37%). This pattern is reversed for seventh and eighth grade students with the first choice of health as a separate subject (42%, seventh and eighth grade) and incorporated with science as the second choice (38%, seventh; 35% eighth).

Health education is also integrated with physical education as a third instructional organization plan for 6-8 middle schools. In the current study, this pattern is present for 13% to 17% of the 6-8 grade middle schools (Table 13), and a pattern of increased integration occurs as grade level increases (13%, sixth; 14%, seventh; 17%, eighth). Figure 7, which details the percentage of basic subjects taken all year by all students in 6-8 grade middle schools, shows that physical education continues to decline for all students all year. This decline may be, in part, the result of health organized as a separate subject and taken for part of the year instead of physical education all year.

Tables B5, B6, and B7 provide the data from the current study for health instruction in the other middle grade organizations (5-8, Table B5; 7-8, Table B6; 7-9, Table B7) and Table B8 for the organizational plans for health instruction in all schools. The patterns seen previously in the 6-8 middle grades schools in the current study are reflected in the other grade organizations and in the patterns for all schools.

READING

As with health instruction in 6-8 middle schools in the current study, there are several organizational choices for delivering reading to young adolescents (Table 14):

1. Separate, with its own period;
2. Separate, but blocked with another content area;
3. Integrated with another content area; and
4. Integrated throughout the total school program.

Reading, organized as a separate subject with its own period, is the most common choice for all grade levels 6-8 (Table 14), and especially for grade six (60%). There is significant decline in its use with the increase in the grade level (47%, seventh; 42%, eighth). Reading as a separate subject, but blocked with another content area, also declines across the grade levels (19%, sixth; 17%, seventh; and 14%, eighth).

This decline in reading as a separate subject, both within its own period and when blocked with another content area, is mirrored in the increase across the grade levels by two integrated approaches (Table 14) – integrating reading with another content area (22%, sixth; 30%, seventh; and 31%, eighth), and integrating reading throughout the total school program (14%, sixth; 17%, seventh; and 18%, eighth).

TABLE 14
ORGANIZATIONAL PLANS FOR READING
GRADES 6-8 SCHOOLS

Instructional Plans	Percent		
	Grade 6	Grade 7	Grade 8
Separate With Own Period	60	47	42
Separate, But Blocked With Another Content Area	19	17	14
Integrated With Another Content Area	22	30	31
Integrated Throughout the Total School Program	14	17	18
Other	2	3	3

Tables B9, B10, and B11 provide the organization pattern data for reading from the current study for other middle grades organizations, and Table B12 for reading instruction in all schools. As with health education, the patterns discussed for reading in 6-8 middle schools generally apply to other separate middle grades organizations and to all schools in the study.

TEACHER PLANNING PERIODS

In addition to examining the presence of teams as an organizational paradigm and the leadership selection process of teams, the 1993 study examined the number of teacher planning periods in middle schools (Table

15, Figure 5). This investigation of planning is of particular importance since many middle schools that are organized into interdisciplinary teams use a combination of both common planning time and individual planning time for team members. Table 15 reports the results of this inquiry for various middle level school grade organizations and the total study, while Figure 5 presents data for teacher planning periods for the total study in a graphic format.

TABLE 15
TEACHER PLANNING PERIODS

Planning Period Organization	Percent				
	5-8	6-8	7-8	7-9	All
All Have One	67	59	69	77	64
All Have Two	15	22	21	10	20
Most Have One	5	5	1	6	4
Most Have Two	11	14	9	8	12
No Planning Period	2	1	1	0	1

Figure 5
Teacher Planning Periods -- Total Study

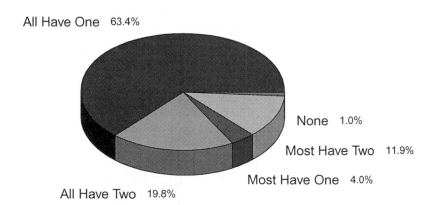

All Have One   63.4%

None   1.0%

Most Have Two   11.9%

Most Have One   4.0%

All Have Two   19.8%

The majority of teachers in the total study work in a school where all teachers have one teacher planning period per day. This ranges from a high of 77% for all teachers in 7-9 junior high school organizations to a low of 59% for 6-8 middle schools. In the other two school organizations in the study, 5-8 and 7-8, 67% and 69%, respectively, of all teachers have one planning period (Table 15).

When the data are examined for all teachers within a school having two planning periods, the 6-8 middle school leads the other organizations with 22%, while the 7-8 school follows with 21% (Table 15). The 7-9 junior high school is least likely of all middle level school organizations to have two planning periods for all teachers (10%). This may be due to the organization of large numbers of 7-9 junior high schools into departmentalized settings wherein one individual planning period is standard. These findings confirmed the pattern reported in a 1992 national study (Valentine, et al., 1993).

When the data for two planning periods are combined ("all have two" and "most have two") (Table 15) 6-8 middle schools are most likely to have teachers with two teacher planning periods with a combined total of 36% (22%, all have two; 14%, most have two). This is followed by 7-8 schools with a combined total of 30% (21%, all have two; 9%, most have two) and 5-8 schools with a combination of 26% (15%, all have two; 11%, most have two). When the totals are combined for two planning periods, 7-9 junior high schools are last (18%) among the four middle level school organizations (10%, all have two; 8%, most have two). Figure 5 reports the results of the total study for teacher planning periods.

Common planning time for middle school teachers organized in teams with additional personal planning time is a basic organizational model for many middle schools in America. Much emphasis in the literature on team organization is placed upon the availability and use of common planning time by the team (George & Alexander, 1993; Erb & Doda, 1989). However, based on the current study, adequate common planning time for teachers organized into teams is still a minority practice. Only 34% of the schools (73% of schools using interdisciplinary team organization) in the total study provide two planning periods for most or all teachers (Figure 5).

Two earlier studies, one conducted one year before the present study (Valentine, et al., 1993) and one in 1988 (Epstein & Mac Iver, 1990) found higher percentages of schools reporting two planning periods for teachers, 54% and 36%, respectively. However, these are percentages of schools using team organization who provide two planning periods. In contrast, the current study reports the percentages of all schools which provide two planning periods for teachers, regardless of the organizational model. If the current study is analyzed using only 6-8 middle schools that have teaming, the percentage of teachers with two planning periods changes from 36% to 58%, a percentage much more like the findings of the other two studies. In other words, 58% of 6-8 middle schools that utilize interdisciplinary team organization provide teachers on the teams with two planning periods.

In 6-8 middle schools, this percentage increases to only 22%. These totals stand in contrast to the number of 6-8 middle schools organized into teams in the core four subject areas (Tables 8, 9, 10, & 11). With almost 50% of these four subject area classrooms organized into teams, but only 22% having two planning periods (for all teachers as well as for the four core subject areas), many must operate without allocated time during the school day to work together, coordinate instruction, meet and confer.

The question of team effectiveness, and this applies only to those schools in the current study organized into interdisciplinary teams, is a question of availability and use of common team planning time. Where it exists, teams have the opportunity to coordinate curriculum and instruction for their common clients. Where it is absent, teams face a daunting agenda of time and effort without support. When teams without adequate common planning time wither, it is understandable.

REMEDIAL ARRANGEMENTS

Middle schools, with their focus on providing developmentally appropriate programs and practices for young adolescents, provide a range of remedial instructional arrangements for students. These remedial arrangements cover a range from pull-out programs in language arts and mathematics or summer school, to smaller scale (but no less effective) efforts such as extra work or homework provided by the teacher, to before or after school coaching sessions. Given the range of remedial arrangements reported by middle level schools in the current study, it is easy to see why the middle school is known as the school that is most sensitive to learner needs.

The 1993 study examined remedial arrangements offered by the various middle level school organizations and the total study. Table 16 reports the results. Schools responded to seven remedial arrangements, many of which were used in multiple combinations. These arrangements covered multiple options within the school day (pull out programs and extra classes), before and after school opportunities including extra homework in the evening, and extended programs such as Saturday classes and summer school.

TABLE 16
REMEDIAL ARRANGEMENTS

Remedial Arrangement	Percent				
	5-8	6-8	7-8	7-9	All
No Special Program	3	4	3	4	4
Extra Work/Homework By Teacher	48	43	40	16	43
Pull-Out Program in English/Language Arts	47	36	28	14	35
Pull-Out Program In Mathematics	43	34	28	14	34
Extra Period Instead of Elective or Exploratory Course	24	27	28	12	27
After or Before School Classes and/or Coaching Sessions	56	65	68	26	64
Saturday Classes	5	6	8	2	6
Summer School	38	46	45	17	45

The data reported in Table 16 for remedial arrangements are comparable for three school organizations (5-8, 6-8, and 7-8). However, in all categories other than "no special program," the 7-9 junior high school was by far the least likely to offer its students any remedial arrangements (Table 16). The relationship between the 6-8 middle school and the 7-9 junior high school on remedial arrangements is elaborated in Figure 6.

The most popular remedial instructional program in the three middle level school organizations (5-8, 6-8, and 7-8) was before or after school classes and/or coaching sessions (5-8, 56%; 6-8, 65%; and 7-8, 68%). This was followed by summer school (5-8, 38%; 6-8, 46%; and 7-8, 45%), extra work/homework provided by the teacher (5-8, 48%; 6-8, 43%; and 7-8, 40%) and pull out programs in English/language arts (5-

8, 47%; 6-8, 36%; and 7-8, 28%) and mathematics (5-8, 43%; 6-8, 34%; and 7-8, 28%). The arrangement of substituting an extra period devoted to remedial work instead of an elective or exploratory course was also employed by these three school organizations (5-8, 24%; 6-8, 27%; and 7-8, 28%). Saturday classes were used by only a very few schools in the current study (5-8, 5%; 6-8, 6%; and 7-8, 8%). It should be noted that the smallest return overall for all categories in Table 16 was for "no special program" (5-8, 3%; 6-8, 4%; and 7-8, 3%).

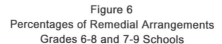
Figure 6
Percentages of Remedial Arrangements
Grades 6-8 and 7-9 Schools

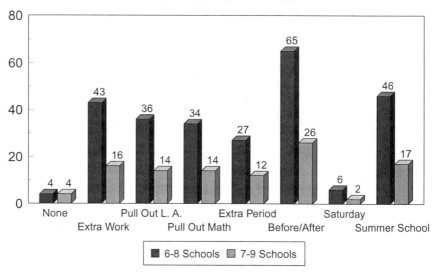

Patterns of remedial arrangements are shown in Table 16. The 5-8 middle school was more likely overall to have remedial arrangements in pull-out programs in English/language arts and mathematics as well as extra work/homework. The 6-8 and 7-8 schools were more likely to use summer school as a form of remediation.

As mentioned earlier, the 7-9 junior high school, in comparison to other middle level school organizations, was less likely to offer remediation in any of the forms the current study examined. The most prevalent program offered in the other grade organizations was before or after school classes and/or coaching classes. Programs in these schools for this time period devoted to remediation ranged from 56% to 68%. Yet only 26% of the 7-9 junior high schools offered this as an opportunity.

Summer school and pull-out programs were also widely used for remediation with students in these grade organizations (i.e., summer school: 5-8, 38%; 6-8, 46%; and 7-8, 45%), yet in 7-9 junior high schools only 17% of the schools employed summer school as a remedial strategy and only 14% used pull-out programs in either English/language arts or mathematics. Such a simple, and time-honored process of extra work or homework was used by only 16% of the junior high schools in the study while the other organizations used it in 40-48% of the schools. Figure 6 offers a graphic comparison between the remedial arrangements offered by 6-8 middle schools and those offered by 7-9 junior high schools. Based on the data in the current study, junior high schools were significantly less likely to offer programs for remedial instruction. The implication for students in these schools who fall behind and need additional work is frightening.

Respondents were asked to list remedial situations that were not included in the choices provided. Typical responses to this option included the following: (a) collaborative teachers offer remediation; (b) peer, teacher, and volunteer tutoring programs; (c) support groups; (d) integrative services; (e) assignments to special remedial classes; and, (f) inclusionary instruction by special personnel and classroom teachers in regular classrooms.

SCHEDULING PLANS

Middle schools have traditionally employed a variety of scheduling plans for organizing the school day. Both the 1988 and the current study examined how middle level schools scheduled their day and the results of this inquiry for 6-8 middle schools are reported in Table 17 for both studies. Four basic scheduling patterns were examined:

1. Self-contained classrooms;
2. Daily periods of uniform length;
3. Flexible scheduling within team blocks of time; and
4. Daily periods, varying in length.

Self-contained classrooms in 6-8 middle schools showed declines in usage at each of the three grade levels between the 1988 and 1993 studies. The highest level of usage was previously at the sixth grade level in 1988. This had declined to 13% in the current study. Usage at the seventh and eighth grade levels, which was already at 9% for both schools, declined to 8% and 7%, respectively. This decline in the use of self-contained classrooms in 6-8 middle schools at the sixth grade level has previously been discussed in reference to the core four subject organizational plans of 6-8 middle schools (Tables 8, 9, 10, & 11).

Of all the middle school organization types that the current study examined (Table B13), the 5-8 school used self-contained classrooms more often than the other school organizations (6-8, 7-8, 7-9), with the most frequent usage occurring at the fifth (30%) and sixth (16%) grade levels. However, the 5-8 school is not the only school that continues to use self-contained classrooms. Self-contained classrooms are employed at the seventh and eighth grade levels in 13% of the 7-8 schools in the current study (Table B13). Self-contained classrooms at the seventh and eighth grade levels may in many cases be limited to special classes since respondents were asked to check all scheduling patterns used in their schools.

The dominant pattern, for all three grades in both studies (1988 & 1993) was the daily period, uniform length (Table 17). This pattern has seen significant growth at the sixth grade level (1988, 74%; 1993, 82%) as well as slight increases at both the seventh (1988, 83%; 1993, 84%) and eighth grade levels (1988, 85%; 1993, 88%). The most prevalent use of daily period, uniform length is by 7-8 and 7-9 school organizations at the eighth grade level where usage reaches 91% (Table B13).

TABLE 17
SCHEDULING PLANS
1988 & 1993

Criteria	Grade 6		Grade 7		Grade 8	
	1988	1993	1988	1993	1988	1993
Self-Contained Classroom	20	13	9	8	9	7
Daily Periods - Uniform Length	74	82	83	84	85	88
Flexible Scheduling Within Blocks for Teams	30	40	25	40	21	27
Daily Periods - Varying In Length	12	6	11	5	10	5

1988: Grades 6-8 schools
1993: Grades 6-8 schools

From 1988 to 1993 there was a significant increase in the use of flexible scheduling within blocks for teams at all three grade levels in 6-8 middle schools. This increase was most visible at the sixth (1988, 30%; 1993, 40%) and seventh (1988, 25%; 1993, 40%) grade levels, with a smaller increase coming at the eighth grade level (1988, 21%; 1993,

27%). These data, coupled with that previously discussed concerning the use of interdisciplinary team organization for the core four subject areas (Tables 8, 9, 10, & 11), demonstrate the continuing growth of team organizations with flexible control over daily schedules.

The fourth scheduling plan that was examined by both the 1988 and the current study, the use of daily periods of varying length in 6-8 middle schools, showed a decline at all three grade levels between the two studies. In each case, the decline was approximately 50% – from 12% to 6% at the sixth grade level, 11% to 5% at the seventh grade level, and 10% to 5% at the eighth grade level (Table 17). □

5.

CURRICULUM

A *critical characteristic of the exemplary middle school is its comprehensive curriculum; that is, the program of planned learning opportunities for its students* (George & Alexander, 1993, p. 55).

The "program of planned learning opportunities" was one of several major foci in the 1993 survey. The survey asked middle schools about their curriculum in broad terms ("planned learning opportunities"), not just in terms of the courses or subjects in which young adolescents were enrolled. This chapter examines five areas of the middle school:

- Basic subjects taken all year by all students
- Required and elective course offerings
- Length of time for selected courses
- Selected student activities
- Interest class/mini-course programs

BASIC SUBJECTS TAKEN ALL YEAR BY ALL STUDENTS

The middle school curriculum has a mission of "general education" for all its clients (Beane, 1993). This emphasis on general education can be seen in the focus upon basic subjects taken all year by all students (Table 18). In the basic subject areas of language arts, mathematics, science, and social studies (often referred to as the core four in middle school literature), an overwhelming percentage of the 6-8 middle school respondents indicated that all students took these subjects all year. This pattern of general education preparation continues at the same extraordinary level that Alexander and McEwin reported in 1988.

The 6-8 middle schools in the current study reported that all students were enrolled all year at the following levels in the core four subject areas:

- 99% in language arts classes;
- 100% in mathematics classes;
- 95% in science classes;
- 97% in social studies classes.

Between 1988 and 1993 there was a noticeable decrease in the number of 6-8 middle schools in which all students were enrolled all year in physical education (Table 18). In 1993 the percentage was 75%, a figure which encompassed a significant majority of young adolescents. However, this figure had decreased 5% (1988, 80%) from the 1988 study. This decline (and the lower percentage of enrollment compared to the core four subjects) may be the result of various patterns of physical education and health curriculum offerings in the middle school (i.e., alternating quarters or semesters of physical education and health or alternating days of physical education and health).

TABLE 18
BASIC SUBJECTS TAKEN ALL
YEAR BY ALL STUDENTS
1988 & 1993

Subjects	Percent	
	1988	1993
Language Arts	99	99
Mathematics	100	100
Science	94	95
Social Studies	96	97
Physical Education	80	75

1988: Grades 6-8 schools
1993: Grades 6-8 schools

Figure 7 provides a graphic comparison of the data from the 1988 and 1993 surveys on the percentage of basic subjects taken all year by all students in 6-8 middle schools. In the core four subjects there were only increases, albeit small ones (science: 1988, 94%; 1993, 95%) (social studies: 1988, 96%; 1993, 97%). The decrease in physical education (1988, 80%; 1993, 75%) is not yet a trend, and further investigation over time will be needed before any conclusions concerning physical education and its status as a basic subject can be validly made.

Table C1 reports the data for basic subjects taken all year by all students in the total study. Language arts and mathematics were the leaders with 99% of all schools in the current study enrolling all students all year in these two basic subjects. Social studies followed at the 97% level with science completing the core four subjects for all students all year at the 93% level. Physical education continued the pattern that was seen in the 6-8 middle schools in this study (Table 18, Figure 7) and enrolled 75% of all students all year for all of the schools.

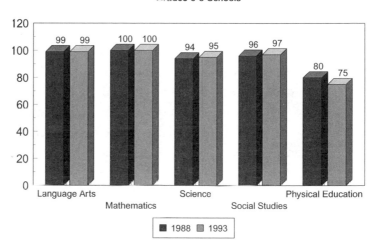

Figure 7
Percentages of Basic Subjects Taken All Year By All Students
Grades 6-8 Schools

The 5-8 school had the highest levels of student enrollment for all students taking the five basic subjects all year. Students in these schools were enrolled at the following levels:
- 100% in language arts;
- 100 % in mathematics;
- 98% in science;
- 99% in social studies; and
- 83% in physical education.

Of all the school organizations in the current study (5-8, 6-8, 7-8, and 7-9) the 7-9 junior high school was the only organization with a significant variance in its basic subject enrollment from other middle school organizations, that variance coming in the subject areas of science and physical education. In science, 81% of the 7-9 junior high schools in the current study enrolled all students all year. The other school organizations had significantly higher percentages of enrollment in science by all students, all year (5-8, 98%; 6-8, 95%; 7-8, 91%).

The pattern observed in science was also visible in physical education. In the 7-9 junior high schools in the current study, 64% enrolled all students in physical education all year. This figure was a significant departure from the enrollment levels of the 5-8, 6-8, and 7-8 schools in the current study (5-8, 83%; 6-8 & 7-8, 75%).

REQUIRED AND ELECTIVE COURSE OFFERINGS

While the vast majority of young adolescents who attended middle level schools in the current study were enrolled in the basic subjects of language arts, mathematics, science, social studies, and physical education, these comprised but a portion of their "program of planned learning opportunities." The 1993 survey, as in 1988, examined the required and elective courses that were offered to young adolescents in middle level schools. Table 19 reports the results of this investigation for grades 6-8 middle schools for both the 1988 and the 1993 studies.

There was a significant range of offerings to young adolescents as both required and elective course in 6-8 middle schools. Several course offerings showed significant gains from 1988 to the current study, while others showed significant decreases (Table 19).

The most frequently required courses at the 6th grade level and the percentage change from 1988 to the current study were: reading, 80% (5% decrease); health, 65% (6% increase); art, 63% (4% decrease); general music, 45% (4% decrease); sex education, 42% (19% increase); computers, 42% (4% increase); home economics, 33% (1% decrease); and industrial arts, 31% (5% decrease).

At the 7th grade level the most frequently required courses (and the percentage change) were: health, 68% (10% increase); reading, 62% (8% decrease); sex education, 45% (18% increase); art, 44% (2% decrease); computers, 41% (1% increase); home economics, 36% (1% increase); and industrial arts, 34% (4% decrease).

The 8th grade level in the 6-8 schools in the current study offered the following courses most frequently: health, 68% (11% increase); reading, 54% (4% decrease); sex education, 44% (18% increase); computers, 35% (2% decrease); art, 33% (1% decrease); home economics, 30% (no change); and industrial arts, 30% (1% increase).

There was a significant difference at all three grade levels in the elective offerings of 6-8 middle schools when compared to the required offerings. The following discussion covers each grade level's most frequent elective course offerings and the percentage change for that elective offering between 1988 and 1993 (Table 19).

The most frequently offered electives at the 6th grade level in the current study were: band, 90% (no 1988 data); chorus, 61% (no 1988 data); orchestra, 36% (no 1988 data); art, 32% (10% increase); general music, 23% (6% increase); computers, 20% (9% increase). The most frequently offered courses at the 7th grade level were: band, 93% (no 1988 data); chorus, 76% (no 1988 data); art, 47%, (6% increase); orchestra, 38%, (no 1988 data); foreign language, 37% (8% increase); industrial arts, 34% (2% increase); home economics, 33% (no change); computers, 31% (12% increase).

Elective options for 8th graders were offered with the following frequencies: band, 94% (no 1988 data); chorus, 79% (no 1988 data); art, 56% (4% increase); foreign language, 51% (9% increase); industrial arts, 45% (2% decrease); home economics, 44% (3% decrease); computers, 39% (14% increase); orchestra, 39% (no 1988 data).

Based on a review of the data in Table 19, there are particular patterns for various courses both as requirements and electives across the grade levels and across the two studies (1988 and 1993) for 6-8 middle schools. For example, art, computers, foreign language, and sex education, when offered as electives, have increased at each of the three grade levels. Health and foreign language have exhibited this same pattern when they are required course offerings, while reading as a required course shows declines between 1988 and the current study at all three grade levels, as well as a decline in offering as one moves from the sixth to the eighth grade. Three subject offerings, creative writing, home economics, and industrial arts show stability across the three grade levels and over the two studies.

Patterns similar to the above discussion are visible when the data for required and elective course offerings are reviewed for all schools in the current study (5-8, 6-8, 7-8, and 7-9) (Table C5). For example, art reflects a decline across the grade levels as a required course as one moves from 5th grade to 8th grade, and manifests the reverse when seen as an elective subject (art as a required course: 5th, 74%; 6th, 61%; 7th, 45%; 8th, 33%) (art as an elective course: 5th 14%; 6th, 28%; 7th, 53%; 8th, 54%). While this decrease/increase pattern is occurring, the total percentage of schools offering art (as both required and elective offerings) remains fairly stable across the grade levels (5th, 88%; 6th 89%; 7th 98%; 8th 87%). Similar patterns for other offerings across the grade levels can be seen, for both requirements and electives, in Table C5.

TABLE 19
REQUIRED AND ELECTIVE COURSE OFFERINGS
GRADES 6-8 SCHOOLS -- 1988 & 1993

Course	Percent					
	Grade 6		Grade 7		Grade 8	
	'88	'93	'88	'93	'88	'93
Agriculture Required	1	1	1	1	1	1
Elective	0	1	0	3	2	5
Art Required	63	59	46	44	34	33
Elective	22	32	41	47	52	56
Band Required	--	--	--	--	--	--
Elective	--	90	--	93	--	94
Careers Required	6	9	9	12	12	18
Elective	4	9	7	12	10	16
Chorus Required	--	--	--	--	--	--
Elective	--	61	--	76	--	79
Computers Required	38	42	40	41	37	35
Elective	11	20	19	31	25	39
Creative Writing Required	23	23	23	25	24	25
Elective	3	4	5	8	6	10
Foreign Language Required	8	16	10	15	8	14
Elective	12	16	29	37	42	51
General Music Required	49	45	31	29	21	21

TABLE 19 (CON'T.)

Course	Percent					
	Grade 6		Grade 7		Grade 8	
	'88	'93	'88	'93	'88	'93
General Music Elective	17	23	20	23	21	21
Health Required	59	65	58	68	57	68
Elective	1	5	3	6	3	7
Home Economics Required	34	33	35	36	30	30
Elective	10	16	33	33	47	44
Industrial Arts Required	36	31	38	34	29	30
Elective	10	16	32	34	47	45
Journalism Required	--	--	--	--	--	--
Elective	3	7	11	16	16	27
Orchestra Required	--	--	--	--	--	--
Elective	--	36	--	38	--	39
Reading Required	85	80	70	62	58	54
Elective	1	5	5	10	10	12
Sex Education Required	23	42	27	45	26	44
Elective	3	5	5	6	5	6
Speech Required	5	7	6	8	6	7
Elective	4	7	8	12	11	15
Typing Required	6	8	4	6	5	14
Elective	4	5	9	11	13	14

LENGTH OF TIME FOR SELECTED COURSES

While the required and elective course offerings of middle level schools provide insights into the curriculum that young adolescents experience, information concerning the length of time that young adolescents experience these courses is also of importance. The 1993 study examined the issue of course length for required and elective courses by asking respondents to indicate whether the courses were offered for a full year, one-half year, or less than one-half year. Data are reported for selected courses at the 7th grade in grades 6-8 middle schools in Table 20.

TABLE 20
LENGTH OF TIME FOR SELECTED SEVENTH GRADE COURSES
GRADES 6-8 SCHOOLS

Courses	Percent		
	Year	One-Half Year	Less Than One-Half Year
Band	90	8	2
Orchestra	86	10	3
Reading	86	9	5
Chorus	73	18	9
Creative Writing	58	14	27
Foreign Language	48	27	26
Journalism	38	28	33
Speech	28	30	42
General Music	24	29	47
Health	21	29	50
Art	16	34	50
Computers	15	33	52
Careers	13	27	60
Typing	13	43	43
Industrial Arts	12	35	52
Home Economics	10	35	55
Sex Education	9	11	80
Agriculture	7	34	59

Three patterns emerge from the data for the selected 7th grade course offerings:

1. One group of courses were offered by a significant number of 6-8 schools in the current study at the 7th grade level for the entire year. These courses were traditional large-group music performance courses and reading (band, 90%; orchestra, 86%; reading, 86%; chorus, 73%).

2. A second group of courses clustered around the "less than one-half year" time frame (a time frame that commends itself to a 6 or 9 week rotating wheel schedule) and reflect both traditional elective offerings at the middle level with some relatively new courses (sex education, 80%; careers, 60%; home economics, 55%; computers, 52%; industrial arts, 52%; health, 50%; art, 50%).

3. A relatively small percentage (generally 33% or less) of the 6-8 middle schools in the current study employed a semester-long approach to required or elective course offerings at the 7th grade level.

These three patterns hold true when data from 5-8 middle schools and all schools in the current study are examined (Tables C6 and C9).

SELECTED STUDENT ACTIVITIES

Planned learning experiences encompass more than required and elective subjects. The current study examined selected student activities in 6-8 middle schools in order to understand the broad range of curricular offerings for young adolescents in middle schools. Table 21 reports the results of this inquiry for 6-8 middle schools in the current study.

TABLE 21
SELECTED STUDENT ACTIVITIES
GRADES 6-8 SCHOOLS

Activity	Percent		
	Grade 6	Grade 7	Grade 8
Honor Society	20	41	46
Publications	37	49	63
Student Council	85	85	89
Social Dancing	56	65	67
School Parties	70	67	68

Student councils were the most frequently used student activity at all grade levels in 6-8 middle schools in the current study followed by school parties. There was a small increase in the number of schools using student councils as the grade levels progress from 6th through 8th grade (6th grade, 85%; 7th grade, 85%; 8th grade, 89%) while school parties demonstrated a small decline (6th, 70%; 7th, 67%; 8th, 68%). Publications, honor society, and social dancing show significant gains across the grade levels. Publications increases from 37% of the 6-8 middle schools offering it as a student activity at the 6th grade level to 63% at the 8th grade. Honor society increased 26% from 6th to 8th grade (6th grade, 20%; 7th grade, 41%; 8th grade 46%), while social dancing increased 11% (6th grade, 56%; 7th grade, 65%; 8th grade, 67%).

When data for 5-8 schools are examined for selected student activities, a split between 5th/6th and 7th/8th is visible (Table C10). For example, publications were offered at the 5th and 6th grade level at 24% and 29% respectively, yet jumped to 44% and 52% at the 7th and 8th grade levels. This pattern can be seen with other student activities for 5-8 schools.

Table C13 provides data for all schools in the current study for selected student activities. These data clearly illustrate that the 8th grade level is the predominant grade level for selected student activities to be offered with the exception of school parties (this is most frequently offered at the 5th grade level in 5-8 schools).

INTEREST CLASS/MINI-COURSE PROGRAMS

The current study asked respondents to indicate whether or not they had an interest class/mini-course program. The survey instrument defined an interest class/mini-course as "a short-term, student interest-centered course." Respondents with such programs were also asked to indicate the number of days per week such courses met and the number of weeks for the mini-course. Data from these planned learning experiences are reported in Tables 22, 23 and 24 and Figure 8.

Table 22 reports the percentage of schools, by grade organization, that offered mini-courses. Both 5-8 and 6-8 schools were more likely to offer such programs (5-8 and 6-8, 34%), while 7-8 and 7-9 schools were less likely to offer them (7-8, 26%; 7-9, 22%). Overall, 31% of schools in the total study offered mini-course programs (Table 22).

TABLE 22
INTEREST CLASS/MINI-
COURSE PROGRAMS

Grade Organization	Percent
5-8	34
6-8	34
7-8	26
7-9	22
All	31

Schools that offered mini-course programs reported their frequency in days per week (Table 23). Five days per week was the most popular offering, followed by one and two days per week. A very small percentage of schools used a pattern of three or four days per week.

TABLE 23
FREQUENCY OF INTEREST CLASS/
MINI-COURSE OFFERINGS

Days Per Week	Percent				
	5-8	6-8	7-8	7-9	All
5	51	47	54	57	48
4	2	5	7	4	5
3	6	9	7	4	8
2	11	14	11	14	13
1	30	26	21	21	26

Five days per week was used by 48% of the schools in the total study with mini-course programs (5-8, 51%; 6-8, 47%; 7-8, 54%; 7-9, 57%) with one day per week employed by 26% of schools in the total study (5-8, 30%; 6-8, 26%; 7-8, 21%; 7-9, 21%). Figure 8 provides a graphical representation of the frequency of mini-course offerings for the total study.

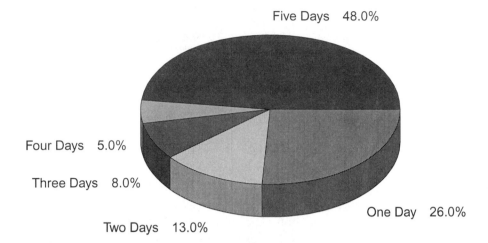

Figure 8
Frequency of Interest Course/Mini-Course Offerings
Total Study

Five Days   48.0%

Four Days   5.0%

Three Days   8.0%

Two Days   13.0%

One Day   26.0%

TABLE 24
LENGTH OF INTEREST CLASS/
MINI-COURSE OFFERINGS

Number of Weeks	Percent				
	5-8	6-8	7-8	7-9	All
1- 3	4	8	8	14	8
4- 6	40	28	28	17	29
7- 9	30	38	46	38	39
10-12	10	11	10	21	11
13-15	0	1	1	0	1
16-18	2	7	2	3	5
19+	14	7	4	7	7

The most popular length of mini-course offerings for those schools with this program varied among the school organizations, but was either 4-6 or 7-9 weeks with the exception of the 7-9 junior high school (Table 24). The most popular pattern overall was 7-9 weeks (39%), followed by 4-6 weeks (29%). The 5-8 schools most frequently employed mini-courses of 4-6 weeks, followed by 7-9 weeks. The 6-8 and 7-8 school reversed that pattern and the 7-9 junior high school used 7-9 weeks followed by 10-12 weeks.□

6.

INSTRUCTION AND REPORTING PUPIL PROGRESS

Much of the visible work of middle schools is the daily instruction that students receive and how well they master the knowledge, skills, and dispositions contained in these instructional activities. This chapter examines three elements important to middle schools in instruction and student reporting:

- Estimated levels of use of interdisciplinary instruction;
- Frequency of use of selected instructional strategies; and,
- Student progress reporting.

ESTIMATES OF IMPLEMENTATION LEVELS OF INTERDISCIPLINARY INSTRUCTION

Table 25 provides data from the 1993 study on estimates of the percentages of interdisciplinary instruction utilized in middle level schools (5-8, 6-8, 7-8, and 7-9). The vast majority (approximately 60%) of all school types estimated that they used interdisciplinary instruction from 1-20% of the time. For the schools using interdisciplinary instruction more than 20% of the time the percentage decreased dramatically. Approximately 25% of the schools estimated usage of interdisciplinary instruction from 21-40% of the time. Beyond this point (41-100%), a very small percentage of any school organization (5-8, 6-8, 7-8, and 7-9) reported using interdisciplinary instruction (Table 25).

The various school organizations (5-8, 6-8, 7-8, and 7-9) are comparable in their estimates of use of interdisciplinary instruction (Table 25). The largest estimated percentage of interdisciplinary instruction for 1-20% of the time was made by respondents from 7-9 junior high schools (69%). This was followed by 5-8 schools (63%), 7-8 schools (61%), and 6-8 schools (57%). Overall, respondents from 60% of all schools estimated that interdisciplinary instruction was used in their schools from 1-20% of the time.

The relative position of the various school organizations changed slightly as the percentage of estimated use increased to 21-40%. Twenty-seven percent of respondents from 5-8 schools estimated that interdisciplinary instruction was being used at this level (21-40%), followed by 6-8 and 7-8 schools (24%), and 7-9 schools (18%). Overall, 24% of respondents from all schools estimated that their schools used interdisciplinary instruction from 21-40% of the time (Table 25).

TABLE 25
ESTIMATES OF PERCENTAGES OF
INTERDISCIPLINARY INSTRUCTION

Estimated Percentages	Percent				
	5-8	6-8	7-8	7-9	All
1- 20	63	57	61	69	60
21- 40	27	24	24	18	24
41- 60	8	9	6	6	8
61- 80	1	6	6	3	5
81-100	1	4	2	4	3

Combining the two most frequently reported estimates of interdisciplinary instruction from the current study created the following picture:

1. Respondents from the vast majority (84%) of schools estimated that their schools use interdisciplinary instruction, a hallmark of middle school literature, a minority (1-40%) of instructional time.

2. Grades 5-8 schools were more likely than other organizational patterns to use interdisciplinary instruction (1-40% of the time in 90% of schools).

3. Grades 6-8 schools were least likely of all other grade organizations to use interdisciplinary instruction (1-40% of the time in 81% of the schools).

4. Overall, only 16% of respondents from all school organizations (5-8, 6-8, 7-8, and 7-9) estimated that their schools used interdisciplinary instruction more than 40% of the time.

Based on the data from the schools in the current study, it seems that interdisciplinary instruction as a primary instructional activity has not become institutionalized into middle school practice. As illustrated by the estimated percentages of usage in Table 25, interdisciplinary instruction is still something done "occasionally" rather than "regularly."

USE OF SELECTED INSTRUCTIONAL STRATEGIES

The current study investigated how often middle schools used selected instructional strategies. Specifically, middle schools were asked how often they used:

- Direct instruction (teacher presentation, drill, practice, etc.);
- Cooperative learning (structured group work and rewards for achievement);
- Inquiry teaching (gathering information, deriving conclusions); and,
- Independent study (working individually on selected or assigned tasks).

Table 26 reports the data for 6-8 middle schools in the current study regarding the use of selected instructional strategies.

The 6-8 middle schools at all grade levels regularly employed direct instruction at extremely high levels. Ninety percent of the eighth grades in 6-8 schools regularly used direct instruction. This was closely followed by the sixth and seventh grades at 89% and 88%, respectively. When viewed across grade levels, the figures for direct instruction, as with all other selected instructional strategies, were stable across all grade levels (Table 26). It is discouraging to note such a strong reluctance to move away from direct instruction in middle schools. However, it appears that some limited progress has been made in recent years. For example, Cawelti (1988) found in his national survey that 98% of all 6-8 middle schools used direct instruction on a regular basis.

Cooperative learning was used regularly by approximately one-half of the schools (6th, 54%; 7th, 51%; 8th, 49%). Occasional usage was reported by 43% of respondents for the sixth grade and 46% for seventh and eighth grades. Inquiry-teaching reversed the pattern of cooperative learning with approximately one-half of the schools using this strategy occasionally (6th, 55%; 7th & 8th, 56%). Thirty-five percent of the schools reported that they regularly used inquiry-teaching at all three grade levels (Table 26).

Independent study was used by approximately one-half of the schools (6-8th grades, 52%) occasionally. Approximately one-fifth used this strategy regularly (6th & 7th, 19%; 8th, 20%) while 28%-30% indicated that this form of instruction was "rarely" employed (6th, 30%; 7th & 8th, 28%) (Table 26).

TABLE 26
USE OF SELECTED INSTRUCTIONAL STRATEGIES
GRADES 6-8 SCHOOLS

Strategy	Percent								
	Rarely			Occasionally			Regularly		
	6	7	8	6	7	8	6	7	8
Direct Instruction	3	2	2	10	10	9	88	89	90
Cooperative Learning	2	3	4	43	46	46	54	51	49
Inquiry-Teaching	9	9	9	55	56	56	35	35	35
Independent Study	30	28	28	52	52	52	19	19	20

When the fifth grade (within 5-8 middle schools) was examined for its use of selected instructional strategies it looked remarkably similar, as did 5-8 schools overall, to 6-8 schools (Table D1). For example, direct instruction was reported as regularly used at the fifth grade level by 86% of the 5-8 schools. The use of direct instruction at the other three grade levels (6th, 88%; 7th & 8th, 91%) in 5-8 schools at a regular level was also very high. These figures are comparable to direct instruction at the 6-8 middle school (6th, 88%; 7th, 89%; 8th, 90%). Similar comparable data between 5-8 and 6-8 schools are found for cooperative learning, inquiry teaching, and independent study.

Figure 9 provides a graphic representation of the use of these four instructional strategies for 6-8 schools in the current study. The figure can be read either horizontally (follow a time designation such as "regularly" across the four strategies) or vertically (examine each of the four instructional strategies such as "direct instruction" for the time usage of this strategy).

STUDENT PROGRESS REPORTS

Reporting student progress is a significant act at all levels of schooling. Middle schools in the current study employed many mechanisms for reporting student learning and progress to students, parents, and teachers. Data from the twenty-five years between Alexander's original study and the current effort are displayed in Table 27.

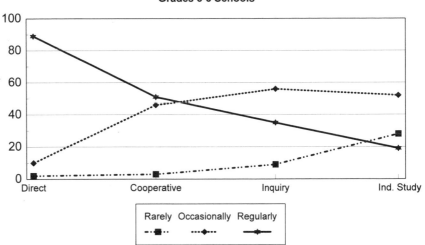

Figure 9
Percentages of Use of Selected Instructional
Strategies
Grades 6-8 Schools

The most frequently used means of reporting student progress over the 25 year period covered by the 1968, 1988, and 1993 studies is the letter scale. The use of letter scales was reported by 80% of 6-8 middle schools. This use of letter scales has slightly declined (1968, 86%; 1988, 85%; 1993, 80%) over the 25 year period (Table 27).

The second most frequently used form of progress reports was that of parent conferences (62%), followed closely by informal written notes (60%). Over the 25 years encompassed by these studies, both forms of student progress reporting have experienced significant increases since the original 1968 study, and slight declines between 1988 and 1993. In 1968 parent conferences were used by 42% of the schools. This increased dramatically to 67% in 1988, before declining slightly to the current level of 62%. Informal written notes experienced a similar pattern from 46% in 1968, to a high of 64% in 1988, followed by a 4% decline to 60% in 1993.

There has been a noticeable decline in the use of other student progress reports beyond letter scales, parent conferences, and informal written notes. None of the remaining forms of progress reports is used by more than 38% of the schools in the current study. This pattern is also visible in the historical perspective from the three studies (Table 27).

Satisfactory-unsatisfactory reports were used by 38% of the schools. While used by a minority of schools, this form of progress reporting has increased significantly since 1968 (1968, 26%; 1988, 39%; 1993, 38%).

TABLE 27
PUPIL PROGRESS REPORTING
1968, 1988, & 1993

Types of Progress Reports	Percent		
	1968	1988	1993
Letter Scale	86	85	80
Word Scale	6	21	20
Number Scale	13	13	10
Satisfactory-Unsatisfactory	26	39	38
Informal Written Notes	46	64	60
Percentage Marks	36	29	32
Portfolio	--	--	22
Parent Conferences	42	67	62

1968: Alexander definition
1988: Grades 6-8 schools
1993: Grades 6-8 schools

Figure 10
Percentages of Pupil Progress Reporting
Grades 6-8 Schools

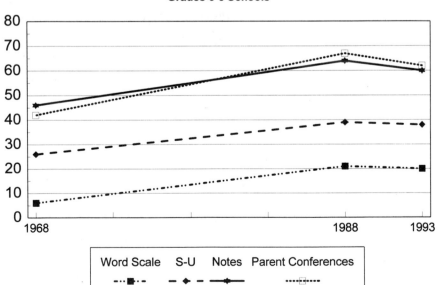

The use of word scales has also increased significantly over the 25 year period. Beginning at 6% in 1968, the use of word scales to report student progress had grown to 21% in 1988 and 20% in 1993 (Table 27).

One form of student progress reporting not included in the 1968 and 1988 studies, portfolios, was included in the 1993 survey. Portfolios, a relatively new form of progress reporting, were used by 22% of 6-8 middle schools in the current study (Table 27). Figure 10 provides a graphic representation of four selected forms of student progress reporting that have experienced significant growth over the span of the three studies – word scales, satisfactory-unsatisfactory, informal written notes, and parent conferences. □

7.
INSTRUCTIONAL GROUPING PRACTICES

The current study examined various criteria that middle schools use to group students for instruction. Comparative data from the 1968 Alexander study and the 1988 Alexander and McEwin study are also reported to provide historical comparisons and to illustrate changes in grouping students over the 25 year period that the three studies encompass.

CRITERIA FOR GROUPING STUDENTS FOR BASIC SUBJECTS

The current study examined criteria used by middle schools in grouping students for instruction in the basic subjects of mathematics, science, language arts, and social studies (Table 28). Six different criteria were examined: (a) achievement tests; (b) I.Q. tests; (c) teacher recommendations; (d) parental input; (e) previous academic record; and, (f) random assignment. An additional criterion (age) is reported for the 1968 and 1988 studies, but was not used in the current study. Parental input is a new criterion that was not used in either of the earlier studies.

There were decreases in the use of all previously employed grouping criteria for basic subjects at all grade levels except random grouping. Between 1988 and 1993, achievement tests as a criterion for grouping students in basic subjects declined from 68 to 70% usage to 44-48% usage (sixth, 24% decrease; seventh, 23% decrease; eighth, 20% decrease). Over the same period the use of I.Q. tests declined by 10-11%, teacher recommendations by 17-19%, and previous academic record by 9 11% (Table 28).

During this period, 1988-1993, the use of random assignment for grouping students in basic subjects increased significantly at all three grade levels. At the sixth grade level the use of random assignment in 1988 was 25%. In 1993 middle schools using random assignments for basic subjects at the sixth grade level had increased to 52%. Similar increases were also found (Table 28) for grades seven and eight. More than half of the schools in the current study were using random grouping assignments for grouping students in basic subjects at all three grade levels in addition to the other criteria reported here (Table 28). The new criteria of parental input to group students for basic subjects was used by 8-9% of schools.

TABLE 28
CRITERIA FOR GROUPING STUDENTS FOR BASIC SUBJECTS
1968, 1988, & 1993

Criteria	1968	Grade 6		Grade 7		Grade 8	
		'88	'93	'88	'93	'88	'93
Age	12	22	--	21	--	22	--
Achievement Tests	17	68	44	70	47	68	48
I. Q. Tests	14	25	15	27	16	26	16
Teacher Recommendation	27	76	57	79	60	78	61
Parental Input	--	--	8	--	9	--	9
Previous Academic Record	15	61	51	65	54	64	55
Random Assignment	--	25	52	24	52	25	51

1968: Alexander definition
1988: Grades 6-8 middle schools
1993: Grades 6-8 middle schools

Figure 11 reports data for seventh grade grouping practices in the basic subjects in graphic form. The changes over the twenty-five-year period (1968-1993) are illustrated as well as comparisons across categories used for grouping students in the basic subjects. From 1968 to 1988, each category saw significant growth (achievement tests, I. Q. tests, teacher recommendation, and previous academic record). (There are no data on random grouping for 1968). For example, achievement tests were used by 17% of the middle schools in the 1968 study at the seventh grade level to group students in basic subjects. By 1988 this criterion had increased in usage to 70% of the middle schools in that study, an increase of 53%. But the use of this criterion (and all others) declined significantly between 1988 and 1993 at the seventh grade level – a 23% decline from 70% to 47% (Figure 11).

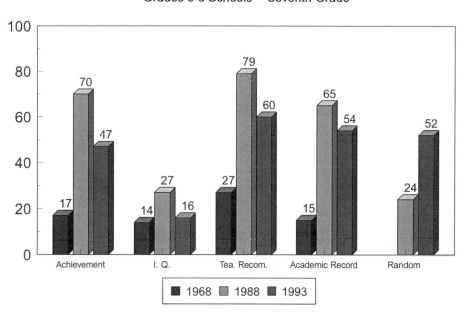

Figure 11
Percentages of Criteria for Grouping Students for Basic Subjects
Grades 6-8 Schools -- Seventh Grade

Currently, the most frequently used criteria by 50% or more of the schools in the current study to group students in basic subjects at the seventh grade level are teacher recommendation (60%), previous academic record (54%), and random assignment (52%) (Figure 11).

CRITERIA FOR GROUPING STUDENTS IN ELECTIVE SUBJECTS

The current study also examined criteria for grouping students for elective subjects in middle schools (Table 29). The criteria used for elective subjects were the same employed for basic subjects (Table 28).

The top four criteria used by middle schools for grouping students in elective subjects were random assignment, previous academic record, parental input (a new criteria in the 1993 study), and teacher recommendations. Random grouping for elective subjects was the most frequently used criteria for grouping students. Over half of the middle schools reported using random grouping for elective subjects (sixth, 54%; seventh and eighth, 55%). Previous academic record showed a significant increase between 1988 and 1993 at all three grade levels (sixth, seventh, & eighth, 18% increase).

Parental input, a new criteria for the 1993 study, was used by 22-25% of the schools in the current study to group for elective subjects (sixth, 22%; seventh, 24%; eighth, 25%). Teacher recommendation, the last of the four major grouping criteria for elective subjects, remained relatively stable over the 1988-1993 period and was used by 18-24% of the schools (sixth, 18%; seventh, 21%; eighth, 24%). Achievement tests and I.Q. tests were not significant factors in grouping students at any grade level in 6-8 middle schools (Table 29).

TABLE 29
CRITERIA FOR GROUPING STUDENTS FOR ELECTIVE SUBJECTS
1968, 1988, & 1993

Criteria	1968	Grade 6		Grade 7		Grade 8	
		'88	'93	'88	'93	'88	'93
Age	12	8	--	8	--	8	--
Achievement Tests	17	8	6	9	8	10	9
I. Q. Tests	14	3	1	4	2	4	3
Teacher Recommendation	27	21	18	22	21	25	24
Parental Input	--	--	22	--	24	--	25
Previous Academic Record	15	12	30	13	31	14	32
Random Assignment	--	50	54	54	55	54	55

1968: Alexander definition
1988: Grades 6-8 middle schools
1993: Grades 6-8 middle schools

COMPARISONS BETWEEN GROUPING STUDENTS FOR BASIC AND ELECTIVE SUBJECTS

Comparisons can be made between grouping students for basic and elective subjects. The following observations apply to these grouping practices:

- Random assignment was the most consistently used grouping practice when both basic and elective subjects were considered.
- Random assignment was the only criteria that increased at all grade levels between 1988 and 1993 for grouping students in both basic and elective subjects.
- Parental input was a more significant factor in grouping students in elective subjects than in grouping students in basic subjects.

- While previous academic record has shown a decline between 1988 and 1993 at all grade levels for grouping students for basic subjects, it had significant increases during the same time period for all grade levels for elective subjects.

RANDOM INSTRUCTIONAL GROUPING

Figure 12 provides graphic representation of the percentages of schools using random instructional grouping. The 5-8 middle school used random instructional grouping more than any other grade organization (5-8, 6-8, 7-8, or 7-9). Of the 5-8 middle schools in the current study, 38% used random instructional grouping. The 7-8 middle schools followed with 36% using random instructional grouping. Thirty-two percent of 6-8 middle schools and only 20% of the 7-9 junior high schools used random instructional groupings. Overall, 32% of the schools in the study employed random instructional grouping practices.

Figure 12
Percentages of Schools Using Random Instructional Grouping

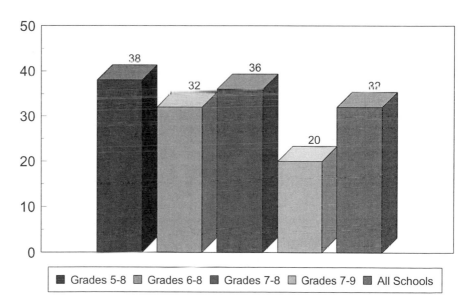

■ Grades 5-8   ▨ Grades 6-8   ■ Grades 7-8   ☐ Grades 7-9   ▨ All Schools

GROUPING PRACTICES FOR TEACHER-BASED GUIDANCE PROGRAMS

Random grouping of students for teacher-based guidance programs was the most frequently used grouping practice in middle level schools. Its use increased significantly between the 1988 and 1993 studies at all three grade levels (sixth, 15%; seventh & eighth, 13%). All other grouping practices (except parental input, which was a new criteria) showed continuing declines from the original 1968 Alexander study (Table 30).

TABLE 30
CRITERIA FOR GROUPING STUDENTS FOR
HOMEBASE ADVISORY
1968, 1988, & 1993

Criteria	1968	Grade 6		Grade 7		Grade 8	
		'88	'93	'88	'93	'88	'93
Age	12	11	--	10	--	10	--
Achievement Tests	17	13	4	11	4	11	4
I. Q. Tests	18	5	2	5	1	4	1
Teacher Recommendation	27	16	14	14	13	14	13
Parental Input	--	--	7	--	6	--	6
Previous Academic Record	15	10	6	10	5	9	5
Random Assignment	--	34	49	35	48	35	48

1968: Alexander definition
1988: Grades 6-8 middle schools
1993: Grades 6-8 middle schools

OPERATING POLICIES REGARDING ABILITY GROUPING

The current study investigated the operating policies that middle level schools used regarding ability grouping. Data are reported for all school organizations (5-8, 6-8, 7-8, and 7-9) and the total study, in both tabular and graphic form (Table 31 and Figure 13).

Three major policies emerged as ability grouping policies that the schools employed to a significant degree in grouping for instruction:
- Grouping at all grade levels in certain subjects
- Grouping at certain grade levels but not all subjects
- Random grouping

There were also two ability grouping policies that the schools within the current study did not employ to a significant degree:

- Grouping at all grade levels in all subjects
- Grouping at certain grade levels in all subjects

The highest usage of ability grouping at all grade levels in certain subjects was found in the 7-9 junior high school (44%). The 5-8 school was least likely to use this policy in ability grouping (23%). Overall, 37% of the schools employed ability grouping at all grade levels in certain subjects (Table 31).

TABLE 31
OPERATING POLICIES REGARDING
ABILITY GROUPING

Grouping Plan	Percent				
	5-8	6-8	7-8	7-9	All
Grouping At All Grade Levels In All Subjects	3	3	4	5	4
Grouping At All Grade Levels In Certain Subjects	23	38	39	44	37
Grouping At Certain Grade Levels In All Subjects	1	2	2	1	2
Grouping At Certain Grade Levels But Not All Subjects	30	24	19	28	24
Grouping Different From Above Alternatives	4	1	0	2	1
Grouping Is Random	38	32	36	20	32

Grouping at certain grade levels but not all subjects was used by 30% of the 5-8 schools in the current study. This policy regarding ability grouping was least likely to be used by 7-8 schools (19%). Overall, 24% of the schools employed this ability grouping policy.

Random grouping was used by 32% of all middle level schools. The highest level of usage was by 5-8 schools (38%), and the least by 7-9 junior high schools (20%).

In comparing grouping practices among school organizations, the following conclusions emerged:

1. The 7-9 junior high school was most likely to group by ability at all grade levels in certain subjects and least likely to use random grouping.
2. The 5-8 middle school was most likely to use random grouping and ability grouping at certain grade levels but not in all subjects, but least likely to use ability grouping at all grades levels in certain subjects.
3. The 7-8 middle school was least likely to use ability grouping at certain grade levels but not all subjects.

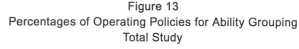

Figure 13
Percentages of Operating Policies for Ability Grouping
Total Study

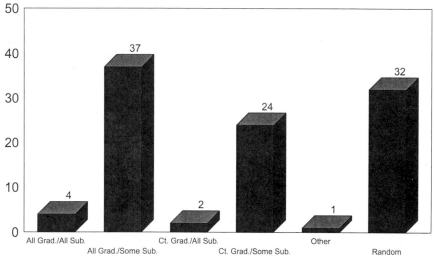

Figure 13 graphically portrays the percentages of schools for the total study that used particular operating policies for ability grouping. For all schools, the most frequently used ability grouping practice was grouping at all grade levels in certain subjects (37%). This was followed by random grouping (32%), and grouping at certain grade levels but not all subjects (24%). □

8.

TEACHER-BASED GUIDANCE PROGRAMS

*O ne of the major dilemmas of middle grades edu-
cation is how to balance the academic emphases
of subject classes with structures that provide early
adolescents with the social and emotional support they need
to succeed as students ... many schools are developing more
responsive support systems, including homerooms, advisory
groups, counseling services, and other activities to monitor
and to involve students in more caring environments. Group
advisory periods assign a small group of students to a
teacher, administrator, or other staff member for a daily or
otherwise regularly scheduled meeting to discuss topics that
are important to early adolescents* (Epstein & Mac Iver,
1990, p. 20).

Teacher-based guidance programs – known under a variety of different names such as advisor/advisee, homebase, and even homeroom – are
a part of the accepted canon of middle school education. Information
regarding teacher-based guidance programs was not collected in the 1968
Alexander study. However, the 1988 Alexander and McEwin study and
the current study did examine how many middle schools used advisory
programs and how these programs were organized to provide appropriate programs and practices for young adolescents. The 1993 survey instrument included a section designed to help determine trends in the number and use of advisory programs. Specifically, this chapter examines:

      1. The percentages of schools of all organizational
           types (5-8, 6-8, 7-8, and 7-9) that had established
           teacher-based guidance programs;

2. The frequency of advisory meetings;
3. The length of advisory meetings; and,
4. Professional staff involved as advisors.

TEACHER-BASED GUIDANCE PROGRAMS

Table 32 provides data from the 1993 study on the percentages of middle level schools (5-8, 6-8, 7-8, and 7-9) that reported teacher-based guidance programs. Between the 1988 and the 1993 surveys, teacher-based guidance programs increased in each organizational type included in the study, with the exception of 7-9 junior high schools (1988, 38%; 1993, 36%).

TABLE 32
TEACHER-BASED GUIDANCE PROGRAMS
1988 & 1993

Percent		
Grade Organization	1988	1993
5-8	41	42
6-8	39	52
7-8	37	42
7-9	38	36
All	39	47

The increase in the percentage of 5-8 middle schools with teacher-based guidance programs was very slight (1988, 41%; 1993, 42%), and the increase at 7-8 middle level schools grew only 5% (1988, 37%; 1993, 42%). However, the percentage of 6-8 middle schools reporting teacher-based guidance programs increased 13% between 1988 and the current study (1988, 39%; 1993, 52%). It is encouraging to note the majority (52%) of the 6-8 middle schools in the current study had teacher-based guidance programs and that 42% of 5-8 and 7-8 schools also reported having these programs. When the total study was considered, 47% of all middle level schools had established teacher-based guidance programs, compared to 39% in 1988.

This increase in the percentages of middle level schools with teacher-based guidance programs is also significant when results are compared with those obtained by McEwin and Clay in a national survey of middle level schools conducted in 1980 (1983). That study reported that only 35% of 5-8 and 6-8 schools had teacher-based guidance programs. Therefore, the percentages of 5-8, and especially 6-8, middle level schools with teacher-based guidance programs have increased (5-8, 7%; 6-8, 17%) during the eight years between these two studies (1980 and 1993).

Cawelti, in a national survey of middle level schools conducted in 1988, found that only 32% of responding schools (5-8, 6-8, 7-8, 7-9, and "other") had formal teacher-based guidance programs. Of these schools, 6-8 schools were most likely to have these programs (38%). These findings are similar to those of the Alexander and McEwin (1989b) study conducted during the same school year (39% of total study and 39% of 6-8 schools). Clearly, the use of teacher-based guidance programs increased substantially, especially in 6-8 schools, during the 15 years covered by the 1980 study (McEwin & Clay, 1983), the two 1988 studies (Alexander & McEwin, 1989b; Cawelti, 1988), and the current study.

FREQUENCY OF ADVISORY MEETINGS

In middle level schools that have advisory programs, how often do these programs meet? As was the case with the 1988 study, the 1993 study attempted to answer this question by examining the frequency of advisory meetings in middle level schools. Table 33 reports the results of this inquiry for the various middle level school organizations (5-8, 6-8, 7-8, and 7-9) and the total study.

The most prevalent pattern for frequency of advisory meetings was daily. For all schools in the current study with advisory programs, 63% met daily (Table 33). Teacher-based guidance programs met daily in 65% of the 6-8 schools. There were similar findings for both 5-8 and 7-8 middle level schools (63% and 62%, respectively). Daily advisory meetings were the operating pattern in 53% of the 7-9 junior high schools with such programs.

However, this pattern of daily advisory meetings declined between 1988 and 1993 for all middle level grade organizations (Table 33). Overall the decline was 15% (1988, 78%; 1993, 63%) for all schools with advisory programs. The 7-9 junior high school led the decline with

25% (1988, 78%; 1993, 53%), followed by lesser declines for the other grade organizations (5-8, 14% decline: 1988, 77%, 1993, 63%; 6-8, 13% decline: 1988, 78%, 1993, 65%; 7-8, 19% decline: 1988, 81%; 1993, 62%). Another pattern of overall decline in frequency of meetings was evident in advisory meetings scheduled twice a week (for all grade organizations except 7-8 schools).

The frequency of meetings that experienced the largest increases was one day per week. This category increased for all grade organizations except 7-8 schools (5-8, 8% increase: 1988, 13%, 1993, 21%; 6-8, 4% increase: 1988, 10%, 1993, 14%; 7-9, 8% increase: 1988, 7%; 1993, 15%; total study, 4% increase: 1988, 10%, 1993, 14%).

TABLE 33
FREQUENCY OF ADVISORY MEETINGS
1988 & 1993

Frequency of Meetings	Percent									
	5-8		6-8		7-8		7-9		All	
	'88	'93	'88	'93	'88	'93	'88	'93	'88	'93
Daily	77	63	78	65	81	62	78	53	78	63
Four Days Per Week	0	1	1	2	0	3	0	3	1	2
Three Days Per Week	0	1	4	4	2	6	5	0	3	4
Two Days Per Week	10	1	8	6	3	5	10	5	10	6
One Day Per Week	13	21	10	14	14	12	7	15	10	14
Two Times Per Month	--	7	--	4	--	5	--	10	--	5
Other	--	6	--	5	--	6	--	13	--	6

LENGTH OF ADVISORY MEETINGS

The current study also examined the number of minutes scheduled for each advisory meeting. Comparative data for this question were also available from the 1988 study. Several patterns emerged from an examination of the data for the length of advisory meetings (Table 34). In all grade organization types between the 1988 and the 1993 studies there was a significant decrease in the percentages of schools that used an "administrative homerooms" time frame (i.e., 1-15 minutes). The decrease was most significant for 7-9 junior high schools with a decline in usage of 43% (1988, 54%; 1993, 11%).

Other grade organization types also experienced significant declines in the use of this abbreviated period (Table 34). There was a 17% decline for 5-8 middle level schools, a 24% decline for 6-8 middle schools, and a 25% decline for 7-8 schools. Overall, there was a 25% decline in the use of the "administrative homeroom" time frame (1-15 minutes) for all schools that had advisory programs.

Along with the decline of the "administrative homeroom" there was a significant increase in the percentages of schools using 16-30 minutes for advisory meetings (Table 34). This was true for all grade organization types in the current study with teacher-based guidance programs. The overall increase for all middle level schools was 23%, increasing from an initial level of 42% of schools with such programs in 1988 to 65% of the schools with these programs in 1993. The 5-8 middle level school's increase was 13% (1988, 43%; 1993, 56%) and the 6-8 middle school increased by 19% in its usage of this time frame (1988, 47%; 1993, 66%). Use of the 16 to 30 minute time frame also increased 23% (1988, 42%; 1993, 65%) in 7-8 schools and 21% (1988, 26%; 1993, 47%) in 7-9 schools.

TABLE 34
NUMBER OF MINUTES FOR ADVISORY MEETINGS
1988 & 1993

Minutes	Percent									
	5-8		6-8		7-8		7-9		All	
	'88	'93	'88	'93	'88	'93	'88	'93	'88	'93
1-15	36	19	38	14	42	17	54	11	40	15
16-30	43	56	47	66	42	65	26	47	42	65
31-45	13	19	10	14	9	14	13	10	10	15
45+	8	6	6	5	8	5	8	31	6	5

Except for 7-9 junior high schools, there was also an increase in the percentage of middle level schools that used an advisory meeting time of 31-45 minutes (Table 34). Overall, the use of 31-45 minutes for advisory meetings increased from 10% of the schools in the 1988 study to 15% in the current study. When combined with its counterpart for the 16-30 minute time frame, this yields an overall figure of 80% of the schools in the current study that have teacher-based guidance programs using between 16 and 45 minutes for advisory meetings.

This increase in time provided for teacher-based guidance in the current study is also encouraging when results are compared to those reported in the 1988 Cawelti study. Results from that study showed that 79% of schools with teacher-based guidance programs provided 15 or fewer minutes per meeting (p. 3), 12% provided 16 to 20 minutes, and only 9% provided more than 20 minutes per day. Further, 6-8 middle schools were found to be twice as likely to provide more than 20 minutes per meeting than were the other grade organizations included in the study.

STAFF INVOLVED AS ADVISORS

Advisory programs in middle level schools are generally staffed by classroom teachers. However, some schools employ a wider range of faculty, administrators, and other support staff in addition to classroom teachers. Tables F2 and F3 report data from the current survey for all grade organization types of middle level schools on two staff related questions in connection with advisory programs: schools where all professional staff serve as advisors (Table F2) and staff other than classroom teachers who serve as advisors (Table F3).

The 6-8 middle school in the current study was the type of grade organization with the largest percentage of total staff participation as advisors (59%) (Table F2). More than 50% of 5-8 and 7-8 schools reported having all professional staff serving as advisors in their teacher-based guidance programs (5-8, 53%; 7-8, 54%). However, only 46% of 7-9 schools used all professional personnel as advisors.

The current study also investigated the area of staff other than classroom teachers who serve as advisors (Table F3). The 5-8 school, of all the middle level grade organizations in the study, used more different staff members as advisors than the other grade organizations (administrators, 41%; media specialists, 48%; resource teachers, 70%; and counselors, 61%). The most prevalent use of staff other than classroom teachers, by all grade organizations, was the resource teacher (56% overall). The second most prevalent group was counselors (39% overall), followed by media specialists (36%), and lastly, administrators, where 27% of the total schools with teacher-based guidance programs used them as advisors. □

9.
INTRAMURAL AND INTERSCHOLASTIC SPORTS

The advantages and disadvantages of interscholastic (interschool) sports programs for children and young adolescents have been vigorously debated since the turn of the century, and especially since the 1930s (Seefeldt &Branta, 1984). This debate has spilled over into the middle school movement as sports programs, along with other activity programs and curriculum components, have been examined as new middle schools are established and existing middle level programs evaluated.

The overriding consideration, when making decisions regarding sports programs should be their responsiveness to young adolescent development. However, making decisions which are best for young adolescents continues to be difficult because of the popularity of sports with family members, students, and others. There is a widespread belief that highly competitive sports are automatically good for all young adolescents. Many family members believe that their children need an early start in team sports so that they can achieve success in high school, which in turn will lead to college scholarships and even lucrative contracts to play professional sports. However, realistically only about one in one hundred high school varsity players receives college scholarships and the chance of high school athletes making it to professional teams is only about one in ten thousand (Beneditto, 1990).

The positive elements of interscholastic sports are often cited and widely believed despite the fact that there is little or no research substantiating these claimed benefits; for example, learning to overcome life's obstacles through sports competition; sportsmanship is learned (Kohn, 1986; Seefeldt & Branta, 1984; McEwin, 1994). However, this does not mean that some of these and related benefits are not possible in carefully planned sports programs.

There is a long history of concerns about the inappropriateness and danger of children and young adolescent sports competition (McEwin,

1994; Sullivan & Grana, 1990). The susceptibility of young adolescents to injury is a major area of concern. It is estimated that about one-third of all sports injuries now occur in children and young adolescents ages 5 to 14 (Findley, 1987). Since 1968, physical injury, medically known as trauma, has surpassed congenital and infectious diseases as the leading cause of hospital admissions and death in children under age 14 (Micheli, 1980; 1990). Other concerns relating to interscholastic sports programs include time missed from school and the growing cost of fielding teams. Intramural sports, on the other hand, are widely considered developmentally appropriate since they provide wide access to middle school students of all developmental stages and readiness levels.

INTRAMURAL SPORTS PROGRAMS

The 1993 survey instrument included several sections designed to help determine trends in the establishment and use of intramural and inter-scholastic sports programs. In grades 6-8 middle schools, 63% of schools had intramural programs for sixth graders, 58% for seventh graders, and 57% for eighth graders (Table 35). The higher the middle grade, the less likely students were to have access to intramural programs (Figure 14). Although it is encouraging that the majority of middle schools now have intramural sports programs, results were somewhat disappointing when compared with those from the 1988 study. For example, 67% of grades 6-8 middle schools had intramural sports programs in seventh grade in 1988 as compared with 58% in 1993, a decrease of 9% in five years. Similar decreases were found at the sixth and eighth grade levels (Alexander & McEwin, 1989b, p. 25).

TABLE 35
INTRAMURAL AND INTERSCHOLASTIC SPORTS
GRADES 6-8 SCHOOLS

Activity	Percent		
	Grade 6	Grade 7	Grade 8
Intramural Sports (Boys)	63	58	57
Intramural Sports (Girls)	63	58	57
Interscholastic Sports (Boys)	26	77	77
Interscholastic Sports (Girls)	26	77	77

Grades 5-8 schools also showed declines in percentages offering in-tramural sports at the sixth, seventh, and eighth grade levels, while approximately the same percentages of grades 7-8 and 7-9 schools offered intramural sports programs in 1993 as they did in 1988 (Tables G1, G2, G3; Alexander & McEwin, 1989b, p. 25). The grade organization with the highest level of implementation at the sixth grade level was 6-8 schools (63%), with 55% of 5-8 schools having these programs at that grade level. Seventh and eighth graders, however, were more likely to have access to intramural programs in 7-8 schools (62%) than in 6-8 and 7-9 schools (58%).

It is discouraging to note the lack of progress in the implementation of intramural sports programs. This period of decline follows a period of 20 years when the percentages of implementation of intramural sports in middle schools increased dramatically, for example from 8% in 1968 to 68% in 1988 at the sixth grade level (Alexander & McEwin, 1989b, p. 23). Unlike the majority of other encouraging findings in this study, the trend seems to be moving in a negative direction with smaller percentages of schools offering intramural programs.

Figure 14
Percentages of Boys and Girls Intramural and
Interscholastic Sports Programs by Grade Level
Grades 6-8 Schools -- 1993

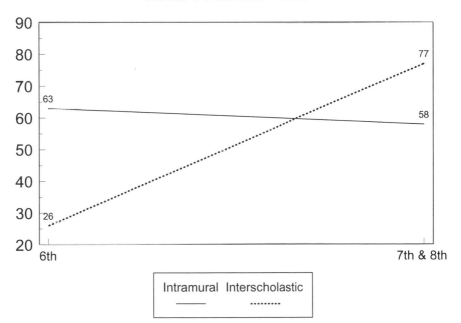

INTERSCHOLASTIC SPORTS PROGRAMS

The percentages of interscholastic sports programs in grades 6-8 schools increased between 1988 and 1993 at the seventh grade level (72% to 77%) and remained the same at the eighth grade level (77%) (Table 35). The percentages of such programs for sixth grade, however, declined over the same period from 30% to 26%. Surprisingly, percentages of interscholastic sports programs at the seventh grade level decreased from 1988 to 1993 in grades 5-8 (82% to 79%) and 7-9 schools (80% to 70%) while increasing in grades 7-8 schools (75% to 80%) (Tables G1, G2, G3, G4; Alexander & McEwin, 1989b, p. 25). When the total 1993 study of 1,798 middle level schools is considered, approximately 25% of schools provide interscholastic sports for sixth graders, 77% for seventh graders, and 79% for eighth graders (Table G4).

These results are lower that those obtained in a less comprehensive 1992 study of 570 middle level schools. For example, the percentages of grades 6-8 schools in that study having interscholastic sports programs at the seventh and eighth grade levels were 89% and 92% respectively (Valentine, Clark, Irvin, Keefe, & Melton, 1993).

The 1993 study included a series of questions regarding changes that had been made in interscholastic programs. Fifteen percent of all schools in the study reported that they had eliminated interscholastic sports programs. Seventeen percent had reduced the number of games played while 30% stated that no significant changes in interscholastic programs had been made in recent years. An additional survey item asked what new interscholastic sports, if any, had been recently added. The most frequently added sports were soccer and volleyball. For example, 291 5-8 and 6-8 schools reported having added new interscholastic sports to their programs. Twenty-five percent had added soccer and 24% volleyball. Ten percent had added cross country, 9% track and wrestling, and 8% tennis, softball, and basketball. Other sports added by 5% or less of grades 5-8 and 6-8 schools were: archery, baseball, bowling, field hockey, football, golf, gymnastics, hockey, lacrosse, mountain climbing, skiing, and swimming. It should be noted that in some instances, sports that were being added were already part of the sports program at other grade levels or for single genders, (e.g., added football for girls; moved wrestling down to seventh grade).

Respondents were also asked to indicate which sports, if any, had recently been eliminated from their interscholastic sports programs. Again using grades 5-8 and 6-8 schools as examples, 127 schools (10%) indicated all or selected sports has been eliminated from their interscholastic programs. Seventeen percent (21) of these schools reported that all interscholastic sports programs had been eliminated. Of schools that had eliminated one or more interscholastic sports, football was the most frequently dropped sport with 19 (15%) of these 127 schools eliminating it. Other sports eliminated included: baseball and gymnastics (9%), soccer and softball (10%), wrestling (8%), and track (6%).

The most frequently offered interscholastic sports for boys in seventh grade of grades 6-8 schools were basketball (82%), softball (73%), and track (69%) (Table 36). The pattern changed in eighth grade to basketball (85%), track (71%), and football (61%). Seventh and eighth grade girls in 6-8 schools most frequently had access to basketball, track, and volleyball. Basketball (81%), track (70%), and volleyball (57%) were the most popular interscholastic sports offered for seventh grade girls.

Figures 15 and 16 show the six most frequently offered interscholastic sports for seventh grade boys and girls for the total study. When all grade organizations included in the 1993 study are examined (1,798 schools), some changes in patterns emerge (Tables G5, G6, G7, G8). For example, football, rather than softball, is the third most often available sport for seventh grade boys (Table 36, Figure 15). □

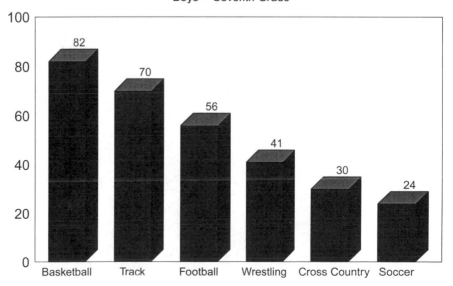

Figure 15
Percentages of Most Frequently Offered Interscholastic Sports
Total Study
Boys -- Seventh Grade

TABLE 36
INTERSCHOLASTIC SPORTS PROGRAMS
GRADES 6-8 SCHOOLS

Interscholastsic Sports	Percent					
	Grade 6		Grade 7		Grade 8	
	B	G	B	G	B	G
Football	9	1	56	6	61	6
Basketball	25	25	82	81	85	82
Baseball	7	1	20	3	22	3
Softball	54	11	73	27	8	30
Track	25	25	69	70	71	71
Wrestling	12	2	40	5	41	5
Swimming	3	3	8	8	8	9
Gymnastics	2	3	3	7	8	9
Tennis	5	5	15	16	17	17
Volleyball	8	16	11	57	12	59
Soccer	11	10	25	23	26	23
Cross Country	14	14	29	29	31	31

B: Boys
G: Girls

Figure 16
Percentages of Most Frequently Offered Interscholastic Sports
Total Study
Girls -- Seventh Grade

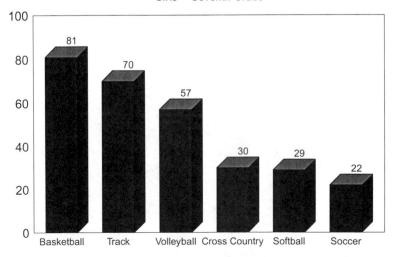

10.

FACULTY

The importance of teachers in any school organization is seldom questioned because teachers are the key players in the success of any school. Middle school teachers are no different. They play crucial roles in all aspects of middle school education – school organization, curriculum, instruction, teacher-based guidance programs, communication with parents, and a host of other responsibilities. One can assume that the more appropriately prepared a teacher is to work with a given developmental group, the more effective that teacher will be. *Turning Points: Preparing American Youth for the 21st Century* (Carnegie Council on Adolescent Development, 1989) stressed this point. According to the Council, if middle schools are to be transformed, expert teachers for young adolescents must be developed.

Although it is generally held that middle school teachers need specialized preparation to work effectively in middle school settings, there is a long history documenting that specialized middle school professional preparation has failed to keep pace with the growth of middle level schools (McEwin & Dickinson, 1995). Furthermore, teachers with varying academic degrees, licensure credentials, and experience are more commonly found in the middle grades schools than in elementary or high schools because of the lack of specialized middle level preparation programs and the specialized licensure requirements that create and sustain these programs (Epstein & Mac Iver, 1990). However, in states which strongly endorse or require specialized middle level teacher preparation, teachers with that preparation are most frequently found in separately organized middle schools rather than in schools with other grade organization configurations, for example grades K-8 and 7-12 schools (Scales & McEwin, 1994).

FACULTY WITH SPECIALIZED PREPARATION

Table 37 provides data from the 1988 and 1993 studies on the percentages of middle level schools (5-8, 6-8, 7-8, and 7-9) with faculty with specialized middle level teacher preparation. Based on the estimates of respondents, there has been little significant change in the percentage of middle level school faculty with specialized middle level preparation since 1988. The largest percentage of faculty with specialized preparation continues to be "less than 25%."

TABLE 37
FACULTY WITH SPECIALIZED MIDDLE LEVEL TEACHER PREPARATION
1988 & 1993

Percent of Faculty	5-8		6-8		7-8		7-9		All	
	'88	'93	'88	'93	'88	'93	'88	'93	'88	'93
Less Than 25	66	57	61	61	57	63	46	64	58	62
25-50	14	19	16	18	16	19	17	18	17	18
51-75	9	12	15	12	13	9	12	6	13	11
76-100	11	11	8	9	15	8	25	11	13	9

Overall, the 1993 study found that 62% of middle level schools had less than 25% of their faculty with specialized middle level preparation (5-8, 57%; 6-8, 61%; 7-8, 63%; 7-9, 64%). Between 1988 and the current study the percentage of faculty in 5-8 schools with specialized preparation at this level declined (66%, 1988; 57%, 1993), while the figure for 6-8 middle schools remained the same (61%, 1988; 61%, 1993). The 7-8 school (57%, 1988; 63%, 1993) and 7-9 school (46%, 1988; 64%, 1993) showed increases in the "less than 25% with special preparation" category, with the most significant increase coming at the 7-9 junior high school (18% increase). Overall, the percentage of faculty with specialized preparation at 25% or less increased from 58% in 1988 to 62% in 1993 (Table 37).

The percentage of faculties with specialized preparation beyond the 25% level continues to be small; in all survey categories (25-50%, 51-75%, 76-100%) the percentage for all school organizations is less than 20%. As well, the changes in faculty with specialized preparation beyond the 25% level between 1988 and the current study is small (Table 37) except at the 7-9 junior high school level where substantial declines

in specialized faculty occurred at the 51-75% and 76-100% levels between 1988 and the current study (Table 37).

Figure 17 provides a graphical representation of the data from both
the 1988 study and the current study for the 6-8 middle school. As noted
earlier, the percentage of faculty with specialized preparation has not
changed significantly between these two studies.

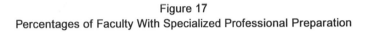

Figure 17
Percentages of Faculty With Specialized Professional Preparation

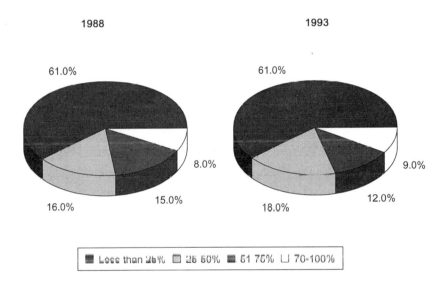

Between 1988 and 1993, the largest block of faculties with specialized preparation was less than 25%. This figure remained constant between 1988 and 1993 (1988, 61%; 1993, 61%). There was a 2% increase in the percentage of faculties with 25-50% of their staffs with
specialized preparation (1988, 16%; 1993, 18%) and a 3% decline in
staffs with 51-75% with specialized preparation (1988, 15%; 1993, 12%).
Finally, for those faculties with a significant majority of staff with specialized middle school professional preparation (76-100%) there was a
1% increase in the five year span between the two studies (1988, 8%;
1993, 9%) (Figure 17).

Based on the data in the current study, there appears to have been
slow progress toward acquiring teachers in middle level settings who
are specifically prepared to work with young adolescents. While the
number of teacher preparation programs for middle level education has

slowly, but steadily, increased since Alexander's 1968 seminal report on middle schools, this increase has not measurable affected the percentage of faculty with specialized professional preparation in the middle level school faculties included in this study.

In 1988 Alexander and McEwin referred to the "alarming fact" that only 13% of middle schools surveyed had 76% or more of the faculty with specialized middle level preparation while 58% of the schools had less than a quarter of the faculty with such preparation (Alexander & McEwin, 1989b) (Table 37). The data from the current study sustains the "alarming fact" that middle level schools continue to be populated with faculty without specialized middle level professional preparation. Other national studies (Valentine & Mogar, 1992; Scales, 1992; Valentine, et al., 1993; Scales & McEwin, 1994) substantiate this lack of specialized middle level professional preparation.

TEACHERS AND THEIR DESIRE TO REMAIN OR LEAVE THE MIDDLE LEVEL

Many teachers of young adolescents today dislike their work. Assignment to a middle grade school is, all too frequently, the last choice of teachers who are prepared for elementary and secondary education. Teachers view duty in the middle grades as a way station. After suffering through a few years with young adolescents, teachers move on to assignments they prefer and for which they feel they were prepared in their own education (Carnegie Council on Adolescent Development, 1989, p. 58).

Since there has been little research dealing with teachers and their desire to remain or depart middle school teaching assignments, the current study asked respondents to estimate the percentage of teachers in their building who wished to leave the middle level (Table 38).

With large numbers of middle level teachers without specialized middle level professional preparation (Table 37), one might assume that many of these teachers would be anxious to depart to other school sites and organizations. However, this was not substantiated by the data in the current study.

Overall, 40% of respondents in the current study estimated that no teachers were believed to wish to leave their school (Table 38). The 5-8 middle school was first in this category with 53% of the schools indicating that they believed no teacher wished to leave the school, followed by

42% for 6-8 schools and 39% of 7-8 schools. The smallest percentage of schools where respondents estimated faculty stability (no one wishing to leave) was the 7-9 junior high school where 18% of the schools estimated that no teachers were believed to wish to leave. Figure 18 provides graphical representation of the percentages of schools where no teachers are believed to wish to leave.

TABLE 38
ESTIMATED PERCENTAGES OF TEACHERS
WISHING TO LEAVE THE MIDDLE LEVEL

Estimated Percentages	Percent				
	5-8	6-8	7-8	7-9	All
None	53	42	39	18	40
1-20	42	53	57	60	54
21-40	3	4	3	14	4
41-60	1	1	1	4	1
61-80	1	0	1	1	1
81-100	1	0	0	1	1

Figure 18
Percentages of Schools Where No Teachers Are Believed To Wish To Leave

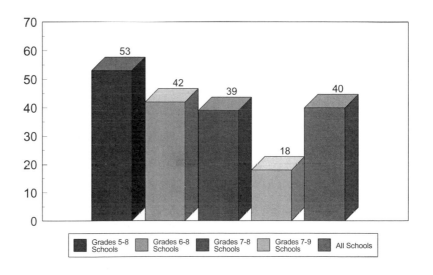

This trend of staff stability in middle level teaching situations continues at the 1-20% level (Table 38). Overall, 54% of the schools estimated that they believed that only 1-20% of their faculty wished to leave the middle level (5-8, 42%; 6-8, 53%; 7-8, 57%; 7-9, 60%). Combining the first two categories of "no one wishing to leave" and "1-20% wishing to leave," 94% of all the middle level schools (5-8, 6-8, 7-8, and 7-9) in the current study had 20% or fewer of their faculties that wished to be teaching at either the elementary or secondary level.

What is most significant from the data reported in the current study is that middle level schools are places where teachers want to be, in spite of the fact that most teachers' original preparation was for other levels. The supposition of the Carnegie Council on Adolescent Development (1989) that began this section is not sustained by the data from the current study or a national study of 2,139 middle school teachers conducted in 1993 and reported in *Growing Pains: The Making of America's Middle Schools* (Scales & McEwin, 1994). □

11.

SCHOOL EVALUATION

A s in the 1968 and 1988 studies, the current survey asked respondents in an open-ended question to describe any plan that they had for evaluating their school. Additionally, respondents provided materials that illustrated such plans. Overall, 903 middle level schools provided information about their school evaluation plans (50% of all respondents). The following provides a breakdown of these responses by school organization: 5-8, 45%; 6-8, 52%; 7-8, 52%; and 7-9, 40%.

THE 1968 AND 1988 STUDIES

Numerous evaluation plans were provided by respondents to the 1968 (Alexander) study. The most common responses included standardized tests, follow-up studies, accrediting evaluations, and self-studies. Several respondents expressed a need for additional evaluation plans while others indicated that such plans were in progress. No respondents reported any unfavorable evaluations had been made or that evaluations were being demanded by school critics.

Respondents to the 1988 survey also found standardized tests, follow-up studies, accrediting evaluations, and self-studies to be popular means of school evaluation. However, other responses that appeared much more frequently than in 1968 included: (a) annual end-of-year evaluations by parents, students, and faculty; (b) periodic evaluations using state-developed and/or other models; (c) task forces, councils, committees of parents, teachers, administrators, and others; and (d) student, staff, and parent polls. The results of the 1988 study led the researchers to conclude that "The generally more frequent, specific and comprehensive replies to the open-ended question on evaluation in 1988 confirm the observation that evaluation of schools has become far more common and better done in the past 20 years" (Alexander & McEwin, 1989b, pp. 43-44).

THE 1993 STUDY

CATEGORIES OF EVALUATION PLANS

The 903 responses in the 1993 study were analyzed and organized into six major categories: national standards and recommendations; regional accreditation associations and standards; state, district, and school evaluation procedures; and no evaluation plans. Because of the large variety of school evaluation procedures, five subcategories were created: testing, committees, outside evaluators, surveys and interviews, and other.

The middle level schools participating employed a wide range of evaluation measures. Many of these were traditional measures concerning student outcomes (i.e., scores on standardized achievement tests, absentee rates), state mandated procedures (i.e., Performance-Based Assessment in Indiana or Illinois' Goals Assessment Program), and regional accrediting associations' evaluations (i.e., North Central Association, Southern Association of Colleges and Schools). However, the schools in this study also used other forms of evaluation that were much more innovative and daring. Responses that illustrate this approach to school evaluation included the use of the recommendations in *Turning Points* (Carnegie Council on Adolescent Development, 1989), and the application for the National School of Excellence program sponsored by the U.S. Department of Education for self-analysis and evaluation.

The following discussion elaborates the various school evaluation measures that schools in the study used. Comparisons with results from earlier studies are made and illustrative comments from individual middle level schools about their evaluation plans are provided.

NATIONAL STANDARDS AND RECOMMENDATIONS

With a current emphasis on national standards from a wide range of educational organizations and associations, it is usual to expect that middle level schools would employ a variety of these standards and recommendations in the development and implementation of programs and practices. Schools in this study also used national standards and recommendations, both those designed as evaluation measures and those designed for other purposes, to engage in self-analysis and evaluation.

School evaluation using national standards, procedures, or recommendations included the use of the Center for Early Adolescents' Middle Grades Assessment Program (MGAP), the National Association of Secondary School Principal's Climate and Satisfaction Survey, *Turning Points* recommendations, the National School Recognition program application, and recommendations from the Coalition of Essential Schools. Comments from schools concerning the use of these standards included the following:

> *We are evaluating our school based upon Turning Points recommendations.*
>
> *We are engaged in self-assessment based on information on the governing principles from the Coalition of Essential Schools.*
>
> *We were recently evaluated using MGAP [Middle Grades Assessment Program].*
>
> *We participate in the Edna McConnell Clark program aimed at restructuring our district middle schools.*

REGIONAL ACCREDITATION ASSOCIATIONS AND STANDARDS

Many middle level schools, like their counterparts throughout the K-16 education spectrum, are evaluated by regional accrediting associations. These rigorous evaluations, involving both self-evaluation and on-site visits, is an effort by the profession to maintain quality control. Attaining regional accreditation status for a middle level school is a significant milestone for the school and its entire school community. Many participants in the current study mentioned the use of regional accreditation as a major evaluation element of their school program.

> *We are in the third year of school improvement and are candidates for North Central Accreditation.*
>
> *We are presently conducting an interim study for SACS [Southern Association of Colleges and Schools].*
>
> *We went through the Northwest Accreditation in 1987 and annually evaluate and report.*
>
> *We are evaluated by the New England Association of Schools and Colleges every 10 years.*

Besides the regional accreditation associations, there are also specific regional standards for middle level schools. The New England League of Middle Schools is active in school evaluation with both published evaluation instruments and sponsorship of site visits by external teams. Middle level schools in the current study located in New England commented about these evaluations, as did this respondent:

The New England League of Middle Schools sponsors an evaluative visitation by a visiting team. We used that process four years ago.

STATE EVALUATION PROCEDURES

State evaluation procedures were common elements in the evaluation methods that middle level schools employed. Schools listed individual state procedures, all with idiosyncratic names or acronyms, aimed at providing a comprehensive picture of a school's programs and practices. Based on the data from this study, middle level schools, like their other grade organization counterparts, follow state evaluation procedures intended to provide the public with "report cards" on individual schools. Comments about the various evaluation measures at the state level included:

We are one of only two schools currently accredited by the state of Michigan and the North Central Association.

We use the California Assessment Program data and Program Quality Review criteria.

Just went through the Missouri School Improvement Evaluation.

New Jersey state monitoring plan currently being revised. We were monitored in 1989.

Blueprint 2000 School Improvement and Accountability system from the Florida Commission on Education.

Our school is evaluated by a state school profile report. This report is given out at a public meeting in October.

DISTRICT EVALUATION PROCEDURES

Considerable richness is noticeable at the district and school levels when it comes to evaluation. Besides the measures discussed above, the middle level schools in this study employed a wide range of standards and procedures at the local level. The reader should keep in mind that district evaluations often look at multiple schools within a grade or developmental configuration. Data at this level are important not only for what an individual school is achieving, but also for how well schools in that particular group are doing.

Comments about district evaluation from middle level schools in the current study included:

The district requires evaluation by improvement in student attendance and academic achievement scores.

The Board of Education is looking for a way to assess the results of change.

District Advisory Board study consisting of parents, teachers, and administration.

Will begin strategic planning in March with other district schools, will look at where we are and where we want to go.

We are in the midst of a district-wide strategic planning which will affect every school.

District evaluation includes a multi-year shadow study.

Periodic reporting to school board regarding various programs.

SCHOOL EVALUATION PROCEDURES

As mentioned earlier in this discussion, the wealth of evaluation procedures and instruments employed at the school level by middle level schools in this study led to the creation of five subcategories for school evaluation procedures: (1) testing, where student scores on standardized tests were used to create a profile of educational attainment; (2) committees, composed of various individuals and representing a variety of groups; (3) outside evaluators, invited by the middle level school to provide an unbiased look at the school's programs and practices; (4) surveys and interviews, either for developing a school improvement plan or to attain responses from various constituencies; and a final category of (5) other.

1. Testing. The middle level schools in this study used a considerable amount of testing in their total evaluation plans. It was generally aimed at quantifying student achievement on state or national standardized tests. Comments from various schools about testing follow:

We use standardized test scores to review programs.

A profile of various indicators (i.e., achievement tests, % of multiple failures).

Use the CTBS [California Test of Basic Skills].

Comparative team data in our CTBS; mastery tests in math and English.

Needs assessment based on test results and other data.

Give reading and math tests at beginning and end of each year.

State assessment testing.

Portfolios, achievement tests, foreign language fluency tests.

Achievement testing for students; item analysis of test data by subject.

Grade eight annual testing.

2. Committees. Middle level schools in the current study used a variety of committees to gather evaluation information; work with national, state, and school data; generate policy recommendations; evaluate specific aspects of a school's program; and work with other constituencies in a variety of settings. Many committees used by these schools were permanent, standing committees while others were created specifically for limited use involving some aspect of the evaluation effort. Comments from the individual schools illustrate the rich variety of school committees involved in evaluation:

Parent Advisory Committee gathers informal but written rankings of strengths and needs.

Established a school Partners in Excellence committee, set building goals, and have district improvement plan.

Shared Decision Making committee is looking into state evaluative tools.

Design team is currently working on several instruments for evaluating sixth grade.

We will be establishing a school improvement team process in the very near future which is based on the Effective Schools' model.

School advisory council organized this year to write school goals that correlate with district, state, and national goals.

We are beginning a committee for transformation study to a more defined middle school.

We have a teaming committee and an advisory committee made up of teachers who evaluate our program.

We have been self evaluating our program using committees to evaluate entire school program.

Currently reevaluating all programs with a committee made up of faculty and parents.

We have established a restructuring committee which consists of parents, teachers, board members, building administrators, central office administrators.

Each spring we have an in-house committee study our current operation and recommend changes.

Intensive self-study next year with staff, parent and student committees for effective middle school research.

Voluntary committees which are currently reviewing discipline; curriculum; parent involvement; mission statement.

Have empowered a teacher committee to evaluate and make change.

3. Outside evaluators. Bringing in outside evaluators to examine a middle level school's programs and practices was used by a number of schools. Often these outside evaluators were college/university teachers and researchers.

We did a three-year study with NASSP's Council on Middle Level Education as the evaluators.

We had a two-day evaluation by middle school level college professors.

Our school and its college collaboration are currently being comprehensively evaluated by university researchers.

A school board team of superintendents evaluates annually.

Recently evaluated by a number of visiting educators.

4. Surveys and interviews. Data collection by teams and committees, outside evaluators, and individuals often encompassed a review of student records, test scores, attendance data, and other forms of "hard" evidence. Impressionistic observations, qualitative commentary, and school image were frequently assessed by other means, particularly surveys and interviews. Middle level schools in this study were appropriately concerned with survey evidence and interviews from teachers, administrators, students, and parents. Community surveys that gathered data from non-parent community members and business people were also employed by these schools. Illustrative comments about surveys and interviews follow:

We use a student survey, parent survey, certified staff survey, and classified staff survey annually.

Send out a parent survey at the end of the year; individually invite all parents into school in small groups over a ten week period.

Student, staff and community responses to oral and written questions.

Currently developing a school enhancement plan based on a survey given to parents, students and staff.

Use entrance and exit interviews.

We evaluate ourselves; parent newsletter for feedback; parent board meeting for feedback.

Staff and student self esteem surveys; school climate survey; parent involvement survey.

We conduct annual parent, staff and student school effectiveness surveys.

Use a pre- and post-school improvement survey that is centered around our school mission statement.

5. Other. Beside testing, committees, outside evaluators, surveys and interviews, the middle level schools in this study used other means of evaluation. These "other" means are described below in commentary from individual middle level schools:

We are currently involved with a university that is instituting a program and evaluation study.

Base evaluation on artifacts, teacher/administrator journals, minutes of leadership team meetings.

Informal evaluation every six weeks.

Yearly school improvement plans developed by faculty and attainment of goals is evaluated by faculty committee.

Periodic faculty retreats.

Teachers evaluate what has been accomplished with our mission statement and our goals.

We have plans to develop theme-based units; stress thinking skills and application and evaluate effectiveness; six units next year.

Annual team leader retreat.

Periodic faculty retreats.

NO EVALUATION PLANS IN EFFECT

While evaluation was an extensive element in the life of many middle level schools in the current study, there were some schools that responded that they were not engaged in evaluation for a variety of reasons:

Still in the process of watching and learning. I have only been here one semester.

Not ready to evaluate, still trying to become a middle school.

So far it has been trial and error.

Looking for good ideas at present.

No formal plans for evaluation of our entire school program.

Working on it.

New structure is at planning stage; presently a middle school in name only.

A COMPARISON WITH EARLIER STUDIES

Results from the current survey regarding school evaluation seem to compare favorably with past surveys addressing this topic. Alexander and McEwin noted in their 1988 study that an expansion of methods of school evaluation had emerged when results were compared to the 1968 study. The richness and variety of school evaluation plans provided by respondents to the current study indicate that this trend toward including, but moving beyond, traditional school evaluation methods has continued to increase.□

12.

PROBLEMS ENCOUNTERED

The current study asked respondents, in an open-ended question, to list any major problems they had encountered in becoming an effective middle school. Similar questions were also included in the 1968 and 1988 surveys. Sixty-seven percent (1,213) of respondents listed major problems. The numbers and response rates for the various school organizations were: 5-8 schools: 116 of 195 responses, 59%; 6-8 schools: 708 of 1031 responses, 69%; 7-8 schools: 292 of 406 responses, 72%; and, 7-9 schools: 97 of 166 responses, 58%.

THE 1968 AND 1988 STUDIES

The problems most frequently listed in the 1968 study (Alexander) included teacher adjustment, finances, and excessive student populations. At that time, "the chief barriers to effective middle schools seemed to be perceived as tangible ones in achieving goals rather than dissatisfaction with the goals themselves" (Alexander & McEwin, 1989b, p. 44). Respondents to the 1988 study (Alexander & McEwin, 1989b) listed some of the same problems reported in the 1968 study, (i.e., teacher resistance and finances). A 1977 national study of 585 middle schools also asked respondents to list major problems they had encountered in establishing their schools (Brooks & Edwards, 1978). Many of the problems reported in the 1977 study paralleled those found in the 1968 study, but a few new ones were added. For example, articulation with elementary and high schools, grouping for instruction, lack of adequate planning time for evaluating changes, and pressure for interscholastic sports activities emerged.

Respondents to the 1988 study (Alexander & McEwin, 1989b) included many of the same problems as did those responding to the 1968 study, for example, teacher adjustment and finances. They also identified problems seldom included in the 1968 study, but found in the 1977 Brooks and Edwards study (1978), for example, flexible scheduling and interscholastic sports programs. Additional problems reported in the 1988 study included: (a) lack of special middle level preparation of teachers; (b) establishing teacher advisory plans; (c) confusion between middle and junior high school programs and practices; and (d) establishing true middle schools.

THE 1993 STUDY

Problems encountered in the 1993 study were categorized into seven major areas: staff, funding, students, programs, parents and community, state and district level, and normal or no problems. Because of the range of comments from individual schools, commentary in one category often overlapped and extended to other categories. For example, many schools listed problems in carrying out effective teacher-based guidance programs (i.e., advisor-advisee, homebase, homeroom programs). Yet this commentary about teacher-based guidance programs was often interwoven with problems concerning middle level school staff and even parent problems, as seen in the following examples:

Parent opposition to homeroom time (see as waste of time); teacher opposition to their advisory role (do not feel qualified or prepared).

AA [advisor-advisee] continues to have problems; teachers tend not to be consistent in what they do.

The problems that middle level schools in the current study face are both systemic problems in K-12 education (i.e., older facilities, inadequate staff development funds, inclusion of exceptional students, bus schedules dictating school hours, heterogeneous vs. homogeneous grouping practices) and middle school specific problems (i.e., the middle school concept, teacher-based guidance programs, interdisciplinary teams and instruction, intramural vs. interscholastic sports programs). The following discussion provides reporting, analysis and commentary on both systemic and middle school specific problems, and uses illustrative comments from individual middle level schools about their problems. In our analysis of problems that schools encountered, there was no discernible difference in any of the problem areas based on the type of middle level school organization (5-8, 6-8, 7-8, 7-9). Because of this lack of problem differentiation, the following discussion applies to all middle level schools in the current study.

STAFF

The middle level schools in the current study identified staff (and a variety of staff-related issues) as the primary problem that they had encountered in moving toward effective middle level programs. For clarity of discussion, staff problems were divided into four subcategories:

- Staff fear, resistance and/or opposition to middle school concepts, programs, and/or practices;

- Lack of adequate staff development activities before implementation and/or lack of ongoing staff development, including lack of graduate middle level education programs and courses;

- Teacher licensure and assignment issues, including shared staffs with elementary and high schools; and

- Teacher contracts and/or union opposition to middle school programs.

Staff fear, resistance and opposition were problems for most of the middle level schools that responded to this question. As noted earlier, this fear, resistance, and/or opposition was often interrelated with other categories of problems – inadequate staff development, inappropriate licensure, etc. However, high on the list of staff problems that schools articulated was sheer opposition. The following comments from individual schools provide a sample of responses on this fear, resistance, and opposition to becoming a middle school:

Staff think no need for change; staff think current ideas will be replaced with new ideas until we go full circle.

Existing staff members who do not have the temperament to teach at this level. We are trying to replace [them] with those who have a background in middle level education.

Traditional belief that teachers giving information is the best way; resistance of junior high school staff to middle level initiatives which makes for a divided staff that is difficult to unite.

Desire to return to good old days.

Getting teachers to use interdisciplinary approach and give up teaching just the facts.

Resistance; apathy; fear of change; older staff; jaded; tried-it-all-before attitude.

Lack of staff development was a problem in moving toward effective middle level programs. This extended to the lack of available graduate middle level teacher education programs and coursework. Occasionally, schools said that there was little or no staff development before opening a new middle level school or converting a traditional junior high school to the middle school concept:

> *Lack of adequate staff development activities prior to implementation of the middle school concept.*
>
> *Education of teachers not available when middle school set up.*
>
> *Antique philosophies; college level courses not available.*
>
> *Resistance to change is encountered only when those involved have not had adequate time to prepare and/or be trained in the changed areas.*
>
> *Usual paranoia people suffer when confronted with bursting the paradigm that exists in their heads.*

Teacher licensure and assignment issues including shared staff with elementary and/or high schools were also a constraint on the implementation of appropriate middle level programs and practices. With licensure, either a middle school license did not exist, or an elementary or secondary license broke in the middle school grades (i.e., elementary, K-6; secondary 7-12) which required two restrictive license areas within a school building. Shared staff with elementary and/or high schools occurred both in buildings with broad grade level patterns (i.e., K-8 or 7-12) and with separate school campuses:

> *No middle school certification; few courses at university level in state.*
>
> *No middle school major.*
>
> *Split of teacher certification.*
>
> *Lack of middle school certification in Tennessee.*
>
> *Teacher certification; specific middle level training.*
>
> *Teachers are either elementary moved up or high school moved down, and philosophies really differ.*
>
> *Desire to block schedule and use interdisciplinary teams while sharing staff with both high school and elementary.*
>
> *Shared faculty with high school (10 miles) and elementary (5 miles).*

Teacher contracts and union opposition, particularly in relation to teacher-based guidance programs, were another source of problems for middle level schools. Representative comments from individual schools include:

Very rigid, prescribed, detailed contract.

Maintain momentum; changing attitudes; union resistance.

Union leadership cautions staff not to agree to changes or restructuring activities.

Inflexible teachers' association who will not let us have an advisory period.

Teachers' union position that advisory is an extra class and pay is sought.

Teachers' union; their bargaining agreement restricts adoption of some middle school programs like advisor-advisee.

FUNDING

Schools provided both direct and indirect commentary concerning funding issues:

Lack of money to support two prep times for development of team teacher project.

No common planning time for teachers.

Funding problems focused on systemic problems of aging facilities, retaining appropriate staff in the face of cutbacks, loss of state aid, over-crowded classrooms, and a lack of technology. Most funding comments directly related to middle level schools focused on the example cited above – common planning time for middle level teachers on teams – and the use of funding formulas for staff developed for departmentalized junior highs and high schools and their programs.

So little time; too many students and too few classrooms causing no flexibility; no common planning time for teachers.

Having the staff, time, and money to provide the programs to meet the individual needs of the middle school student.

We have experienced a gross lack of funding.

Currently facing 4th year of budget cuts; program in jeopardy in order to save dollars.

Fluctuation of staff due to seniority and layoffs; financial instability of district.

Still using an allocation formula derived for junior high school, the formula assumes teachers teach only five classes.

Problems with county office in staffing formula. They don't understand teaming.

School building is over 100 years old.

Funding. We are committed to the concept but need a successful referendum (two failed).

Our budget is tight. Our current department system appears to be cost effective even if it doesn't fit what we know about kids.

STUDENTS

The comments from individual middle level schools focused on three categories of problems:

- Problems that directly involved students in school settings (i.e., lack of productive, meaningful academic alternatives for disaffected students; motivating and involving students; student discipline; and providing for students below grade level);

- Problems that were parent-related (i.e., lack of parental care for some students, or lack of parental involvement in the school); and,

- Problems related to the changing demographics of school populations (i.e., many behavioral, social, or emotionally disabled students; support for at-risk students; high percentages of students speaking primary languages other than English; and inadequate social services for students).

The following comments from individual schools provide illustrative examples of student and student-related problems:

Low functioning students with little or no motivation, usually environmentally deprived.

Discipline problems with chronic offenders also in the juvenile probation program.

Gang related problems on the rise.

Building understanding outside the program of how an environment such as ours is appropriate for troubled youngsters.

Combining students from three different middle schools that have competed against each other into one school and making them get along.

Majority of students are LEP (Limited English Proficient); we have begun the use of writing portfolios to provide for documentation.

Trying to address the needs of an increasing minority population – the language barrier is major obstacle.

PROGRAMS

There were two board categories of programmatic problems that emerged from school responses: school wide concerns and middle level focused problems. School wide concerns involved problems such as involving related arts' staff with core teams; problems involved with schools and teachers struggling with homogeneous vs. heterogeneous grouping; and scheduling students for a variety of programs and classes.

> *I am replacing a principal who was at this school for 30 years and the school is just like it was when he started.*
>
> *Striking a balance between goals of academic excellence and affective needs of pre-adolescents.*
>
> *Due to vast distances, communication and evening events are adversely affected.*
>
> *Eliminating pep club, queens, etc; trying not to have dances; trying to go to intramurals; getting teams started.*
>
> *Making exploratory teachers feel as important as team teachers.*
>
> *Lack of knowledge of effective programs on the part of some teachers and many parents.*

Middle level programs, most especially teacher-based guidance and interscholastic sports, were seen as a focus of problems by the schools involved in the current study:

> *Parent opposition to homeroom time (see as waste of time); teacher opposition to their advisory role (do not feel qualified or prepared).*
>
> *AA [advisor-advisee] continues to have problems, teachers tend to not be consistent in what they do.*
>
> *Elimination of interscholastic sports and school dances in order to replace them with more age appropriate activities.*
>
> *Pressure from high school coaches to form teams rather than intramurals.*
>
> *Sports program is not operating on the success-for-everyone philosophy.*

PARENTS AND THE COMMUNITY

Middle level schools in the current study identified a range of problems associated with parents and the local community, many of which connected with other problem areas. Some parent and community problems were active, as with active opposition to teacher-based guidance programs ("Parent opposition to homeroom time [see as waste of time]; teacher opposition to their advisory role [do not feel qualified or prepared]."), while others came from ignorance or lack of involvement.

Vocal minority of parents who want their children to be part of an elitist "'star' system of education.

Some community members against the school because of consolidation plan that took two junior highs and made one 6-8 and one 9-12 high.

People who feel middle schools overlook the academics.

Community receptiveness to in-depth 'bridge' programs.

Early criticism was that we were not supplying sufficient interscholastic athletics as compared to what is offered in area junior high schools.

Parental acceptance of younger children in school with older ones.

Mentality toward honor roll.

Educating parents.

Reducing elitism.

Parents who want more emphasis on competitive sports.

Parents of above average athletes.

Need more parent involvement.

STATE AND DISTRICT LEVEL

Problems at the state and district level that middle level schools encountered included restrictive state guidelines, mandated state and district policies that conflicted with young adolescent schooling, and transportation policies that dictated schedules. However, the major recurring theme throughout this category was the lack of knowledge and/or support for middle level education at the district level by superintendents, central office staff, and boards of education.

Kansas Quality Performance Accreditation is forcing us into making necessary changes. Frustrated about too much to do and not enough time.

Overcoming tradition and inertia; overcoming low priority that middle schools have had in the shadow of high school and primary school.

No directives from above; no middle school philosophy district-wide; no team time; secondary bias teachers; no commitment to develop middle school program.

School committee, superintendent's lack of understanding about site based management.

Lack of knowledge by superintendent and board in regard to what is necessary for a successful middle school level education.

More mandated programs from New York State have meant reduction in flexible scheduling and interdisciplinary learning.

Commitment to structure but not philosophy; no district middle school advocate.

District doesn't staff for change.

Facilities and controlled bell schedule due to buses and itinerant teachers.

School day length is being dictated by bus schedule.

Curriculum changes are most needed; middle school concept is not understood by decision makers; too much emphasis on test scores.

District refusal to consider housing ninth grade elsewhere.

Transportation need imposed; split of school hours 9-3 for grades 5 & 6, 8-2 for grades 7 & 8.

Lack of school board vision.

People do not understand the middle level concept, public as well as central office staff.

Board of education buying the concept of pure teaming with common planning time.

NORMAL OR NO PROBLEMS

As might be expected, there were some middle level schools in the current study that encountered either normal problems (mainly with transitioning to a new school with a new faculty) or no problems in moving to effective middle level programs.

No major problems, but many small ones; we are continually fine tuning our program.

Teacher cooperation with team members in the beginning; teachers not wanting to be empowered with authority to make decisions.

Keeping staff motivated and enthusiastic after 7 years.

Articulating middle school philosophy is a never ending process.

Smooth, just minor problems.

No major obstacles. The only one retired two years ago.

We made the transition in 1986. Problems then were great but now seem minor.

Change takes people out of their comfort zone.

No major problems; teachers and parents have been supportive.

We are just starting.

Occasional concerns common to any change process.

Just normal [problems] opening a new building with a new staff.

The kinds of problems identified by respondents over the 25 years covered by these studies reveals both problems that have been consistently present since the beginning of the middle school movement and those that have emerged as dramatically increasing numbers of middle schools strive to become more developmentally responsive. A more complete discussion of problems is included in chapter 13.□

13.

EXEMPLARY ELEMENTS AND GENERAL COMMENTS

The survey instrument included several open-ended questions and opportunities for general comments. The information obtained by these survey items was rich and made the study much more complete and meaningful. (Chapter 11 "School Evaluation" and Chapter 12 "Problems Encountered" are examples of what results from the inclusion of these kinds of survey items). The following two sections provide a brief summary of additional data and include selected comments from respondents. The comments included were selected because of their representativeness.

EXEMPLARY ELEMENTS

The survey included an item that asked the following question: "What elements of your school do you consider exemplary?" This question was asked in an open-ended format to encourage respondents to reflect on the elements of their schools that they considered especially successful. The word "elements" was used so that many possibilities were possible without providing choices from a predetermined set of responses. The researchers wanted respondents to reflect on their answers unencumbered by limitations.

Seventy percent (1,261) of the 1,798 schools responding to the study indicated one or more elements they considered exemplary. Almost all schools responding to this survey item reported two or more exemplary elements (average of 2.25 per school). The percentages of the total study represented by each grade organization on this item were: (a) 5-8 schools, 9%; (b) 6-8 schools, 60%; (c) 7-8 schools, 23%; and 7-9 schools, 8%. These results are representative of the total study when the varying numbers of schools within the various grade organizations which received and responded to the study are considered. Fifty-seven percent of 5-8 schools, 73% of 6-8 schools, 71% of 7-8 schools, and 65% of 7-9 schools completed this survey item.

The responses were categorized by the researchers without using pre-determined classifications. The 20 most popular categories that emerged are listed below, in rank order, with the first category being most often listed by respondents as "exemplary." It should be understood, however, that these were not the only categories that emerged, nor are those included in this list necessarily more important than those not listed (1,811 of 2,839 responses are accounted for in this list):

1. Teachers
2. Academic/Core Subject Areas (language arts, mathematics, science, social studies)
3. Teaming/Team Planning
4. Teacher-based Guidance (advisory programs)
5. Family Members/Community
6. Computers and Other Technology
7. Climate/Caring Environment
8. The Arts (instrumental music, chorus, drama, visual arts, etc.)
9. Exploratory/Elective Courses
10. Scheduling (flexible, block, etc.)
11. Test Scores (achievement, etc.)
12. Exceptional Children's Programs
13. The Instructional Program (the total program)
14. Students
15. At-risk Programs
16. Intramural Sports Programs
17. Student Recognition Programs
18. Student Activities
19. Discipline
20. Curriculum (total curriculum).

These categories are discussed briefly in the following sections. The elements are presented in sets of five to aid with organization and presentation. The five most popular exemplary elements identified by respondents were: (a) teachers (21%); (b) the core subject areas of language arts, mathematics, science, and social studies (20%); (c) teaming and team planning (17%); (d) teacher-based guidance programs (9%); and, (d) family/community members (8%).

TEACHERS

Teachers were most frequently listed as exemplary elements of middle schools (21% of all respondents). It is interesting to note that the most frequently listed problem (Chapter 12) also focused on teachers, (i.e., teacher resistance to positive change). This clearly points out the key roles played by teachers and other professional personnel in the establishment of developmentally responsive middle schools. Some sample statements focusing on exemplary teachers included:

> *The faculty provides a good nurturing environment.*
> *Dedicated and hard working teachers.*
> *Collegial support and respect among professional staff.*
> *Staff professionalism and work ethic.*
> *Staff is poised for growth and development.*
> *Teaching staff is very student-oriented.*
> *Conscientious, dedicated, and humanistic faculty members who are open to change.*
> *Strong professional staff who is committed to the middle school model.*
> *Caring and informed faculty.*
> *Excellent professional staff who is enthusiastic about the middle school concept.*
> *Teacher cooperation, dedication, and professionalism.*
> *Professional staffs' willingness to give of their own time to help students.*
> *Teachers are excellent in nurturing, caring, and patience.*
> *Interrelationships among staff and willingness to try new things.*
> *Professional staff members who realize the need for change and are ready for it.*
> *Dedicated and experienced staff who want to be here.*
> *Faculty emphasis on the overall development of middle school learners.*

CORE SUBJECTS

As noted, the second most frequently listed exemplary element was that of the core basic subjects. Examples of responses included:

> *Core curriculum is very strong.*
> *The academic success of our students, especially in the basic subjects.*
> *Implementation of a new language arts curriculum using labs.*
> *Mathematics and language arts.*
> *Accelerated math program.*
> *An integrated language arts program.*

Whole language program.
Advanced science program.
Integrated language arts and social studies.

TEAMING/TEAM PLANNING

Teaming and team planning are widely considered essential to highly successful middle schools. Examples of responses in this category were:

Positive effects of teaming.
Interdisciplinary team organization.
Use of two-teacher teams.
Team teaching and the flexible organizational structure.
Our school is now organized using the "house concept" and our core classes are all taught by teams of teachers.
Team meetings.
Interdisciplinary teams have excellent interdisciplinary units – curriculum integration.
Team relationships.
Implementation of teaming has improved many components of the school including discipline, student attitudes, and instruction.
Interdisciplinary curriculum designed using the team approach.
Integrated teaming.

TEACHER-BASED GUIDANCE PROGRAMS

The importance of carefully planned teacher-based guidance programs for young adolescents has been recognized at least since the early part of the junior high school movement. It was encouraging to find that a significant percentage of middle schools considered their advisory program exemplary. Typical comments were:

A highly successful advisor-advisee program.
Home base advisory.
Our advisement program.
The advisory curriculum.
Teacher-based guidance program.
Advisory program has become the "heart" of our middle school.

FAMILY AND COMMUNITY

The importance of the roles of families and community members in creating and supporting highly successful schools has been "rediscovered" during the last few years. A large variety of positive responses were received in this category. They included:

Strong parent and community support.

Parent and community volunteers.

Parent involvement.

Community service learning program.

Community support.

Parent volunteer program.

School improvement team that includes parent and community involvement.

The parent teacher school association is exemplary.

Wonderful working relationship with the community.

The five most frequently listed exemplary elements are encouraging for the future of middle school education and young adolescents. Teachers and instruction in the core subjects are crucial to success, teaming and teacher-based guidance programs are essential components of highly effective middle schools, and the roles played by family and community members are unquestionably important.

The next five categories most frequently listed, 6 through 10, were: (a) computers and other technology (8%); (b) supportive climate/caring environment (7%); (c) the arts – instrumental music, chorus, visual arts, etc. (7%); (d) exploratory/elective courses (5%); and, (e) scheduling – block schedules, flexible schedules, etc. (5%) Illustrative comments regarding these categories are presented below:

TECHNOLOGY

Technology education program.

Moving into technology in industrial arts.

Computer assisted instruction.

Distance learning.

Technology rich environment.

Computer literacy.

Magnet computer program.
High technology labs.
Teachers' use of computers and other technology in instruction.

CLIMATE/CARING ENVIRONMENT

Kid oriented program.
Community atmosphere.
Positive relationships among the students, staff, and community.
We offer an extremely caring attitude focusing on student success.
Climate and spirit.
Both the academic and the social learning environments.
Wellness program.
Safe school environment.

THE ARTS

Performing arts programs.
Program of the arts.
Vocal music and band programs.
Integrated humanities program.
Fine arts program.
Integration of the arts into the total curriculum.

EXPLORATORY/ELECTIVES

Enrichment/Exploratory program.
Eighth grade exploratory (interdisciplinary and cross-grade teaching).
Foreign language.
Practical arts program.
Health curriculum.
Outdoor education.
Home economics.
Mini-course program.
A good variety of exploratory courses.

SCHEDULING

Flexibility of the schedule.

House concept with flexible scheduling.
Block scheduling.
Flex-block schedule.
Dual track scheduling/calendar.

As with the first five categories, it is encouraging that numbers 6 through 10 represented positive directions toward effective middle schools. It would have been cause for concern if results had indicated that the importance of computers and other technology was not being recognized. It is also encouraging that a significant number of middle schools not only understood the crucial importance of a caring and supportive environment, but considered their environments/climates exemplary. The excellence reported in the arts and in exploratory/elective courses demonstrates the continued emphasis on these areas in middle schools. The reporting of excellence in flexible scheduling is also significant when the importance of eliminating rigid scheduling is considered.

The next five categories, 11 through 15, included: (a) test scores (4%); (b) exceptional children's programs (4%); (c) the instructional program (4%); (d) students (4%); and, (e) at-risk programs (4%). Some representative comments from these areas follow.

TEST SCORES

Standardized test scores.
Our test scores remain high despite other problems encountered.
Scholastic achievement.

EXCEPTIONAL CHILDREN'S PROGRAM

Excellent special needs program for learning disabled students.
Mainstreaming all exceptional children.
Behavior handicapped program.
Learning disability full inclusion model.
Chapter I program.
Perceptually impaired program.
Special education students are mainstreamed and teamed.

STUDENTS

Diverse student population.

> *Outstanding students.*
> *Our students are our most exemplary element!*
> *The greatest element at this school is the students themselves.*

INSTRUCTIONAL PROGRAMS

> *Daily quality instruction.*
> *Inquiry based instruction.*
> *The strong instructional program.*
> *Quality of instruction.*
> *Cooperative instructional approach.*
> *Eight grade integrated unit.*

AT-RISK PROGRAMS

> *The at-risk program.*
> *Student at-risk program.*
> *Our special efforts to work successfully with at-risk students.*

The number of schools reporting excellence in test scores is good news for it documents the academic successes of the young adolescents attending these schools. The exemplary nature of programs for exceptional children and at-risk populations is very positive for it reflects focused efforts to provide opportunities for all young adolescents to learn. It is very gratifying to note that a substantial number of middle schools considered their instructional program exemplary. What could be more important than developmentally responsive instruction? The fact that many schools listed their students as exemplary reflects the student-centered focus of these schools.

The remaining five categories, 16 through 20, were: (a) intramural sports programs (3%); (b) student recognition programs (3%); (c) student activities (3%); (d) discipline (3%); and, (e) curriculum (2%). Some representative quotations from these categories are provided below:

INTRAMURAL SPORTS PROGRAMS

> *Our intramural program is very popular with students.*
> *Our sixth grade intramural program.*
> *Intramural sports are an exemplary part of our program.*
> *We have good balance between intramural and interscholastic sports programs.*

STUDENT RECOGNITION PROGRAMS

Student recognition programs are an important part of the total program here.

Student recognition program.

Student award and recognition programs.

Student and faculty recognition programs.

Student recognition program is popular with students, teachers, and parents.

STUDENT ACTIVITIES

Student activities are very successful.

Success in efforts to involve all students in activities.

After-school activities program.

Extensive club program.

DISCIPLINE/CLASSROOM MANAGEMENT

On campus suspension program.

Classroom management.

Exemplary student behavior.

CURRICULUM

Curriculum (total curriculum).

The language arts curriculum.

Integrated curriculum model.

Curriculum integration.

Categories 15 through 20 also included some very positive elements that were considered exemplary, for example, intramural sports programs rather than interscholastic sports programs. This implies that professional personnel at these schools understand the importance of wide participation in sports activities and programs. Student recognition programs and student activity programs are also very important components of effective middle schools. Citing discipline as exemplary is encouraging and may help destroy the stereotype of young adolescents as perpetual behavior problems. Of course curriculum is always a key focus of highly effective middle schools. (Many of the other categories included comments that dealt with various aspects of curriculum. The category reported here refers only to those listing the overall curriculum as exemplary).

OTHER COMMENTS

More than 1,000 responses not included in these 20 most frequently selected categories were received. These exemplary elements were so diverse that it was virtually impossible to categorize them for reporting purposes in ways that seemed logical. However, the researchers believe that it is very positive and encouraging that so many middle schools reported so many elements that they considered exemplary. This suggests that individual schools are focusing on elements that seem most important to them and, at least in their judgements, are successfully implementing those elements. Some selected comments that reflect the variety and developmental appropriateness of these elements were:

Teacher morale.
The guidance program.
Student led parent-teacher conferences.
No tracking or pull outs.
Service learning.
Museum.
Our mission statement and its implementation.
Adopt-a-kid.
Student assistance program.
Two way language immersion program.
Academic achievers program.
After school and Saturday school program.
Schoolwide bilingual program.
A Japanese immersion program.
Incentive programs for students.
Implementation of a middle school program in a small year-round school.
Publications.
Student assessment.
School improvement through teacher leadership.
Adopt a grandparent program.
School pride.
Shared decision making council.
A mentor site to 48 middle schools.

An environmental club.
Progressive administration.
Ongoing staff development.
Portfolios and alternative assessment.
A violence prevention program.
Applied learning alternative program.
Remedial, special education, and gifted programs.
Heterogeneous grouping.
Twenty-five minutes at the end of the day for staff development.
Incentive programs.
A noon hour activity program.
School television program.
All forms of education under one roof.
Board of Education support.
International studies program.
Cocurriculuar programs.
Lunchtime intramurals.
Intervention assistance team.
Year-round intersession program.
Homework center.
Health program.
Interdisciplinary unit using the "Voyage of the Mimi."
Establishment of heterogeneous grouping across grade levels.
Adopt a student program.

GENERAL COMMENTS

An opportunity was provided at the end of the research instrument for general comments. Twenty-one percent (377) of respondents elected to make comments. The breakdown of responses by grade organizations was: 5-8 schools, 45 (12%); 6-8 schools, 214 (57%); 7-8 schools, 87 (23%); and, 7-9 schools, 31 (8%).

As would be expected in a general comment situation, the responses were diverse and covered a wide range of topics.

Several comments addressed professional associations:

*Thanks to National Middle School Association, our commitment
to becoming a model middle school is becoming a reality.*
We are active in the Virginia Middle School Association.

Other comments focused on the progress made by schools and what needed to be accomplished in the future:

Beginning to move toward greater cooperation and changing from a junior high school model to a middle school model.

We are implementing team teaching in all disciplines and exposing students to new experiences.

We have made significant changes to promote teaming, but we still have a long way to go.

Over the next three years we are going to offer students, parents, and teachers organizational options (multigrades, teams, self-contained, etc.) in grades 5-8.

I want this school to change. We have a very traditional school. My vision is for it to become a more progressive school in the near future.

We have a long way to go before we achieve the middle school we envision is best for students. We are in the first year of this process.

Still others lamented the current situation of their schools as demonstrated in Chapter 12, "Problems Encountered."

School has undergone very frequent turnover in administrators in the last 20 years, so very few programs are creative and beneficial to students.

Middle school in name only.

Movement is slow with a secondary oriented staff.

Our middle schools have suffered from transition from a junior high school to a middle school rather than "stopping" the junior high school model and "starting" a middle school model.

Amazed at how difficult change is at the middle level—subject ownership rather than student ownership.

We are moving without significant success. The overall 7-9 grade structure makes it very difficult.

Other respondents included positive statements about accomplishments at their schools:

Ninety-nine percent of all students made passing grades last year.

The middle school concept works. We are forming teams of teachers, families, and heterogeneous grouping.

We have been selected by the Texas Education Agency as a mentor middle school (39 were selected out of 1500).

We allow all students who wish to do so participate in cheerleading and a series of one-act plays.

The grades 7-8 middle school organization was so successful that we are adding grade six next year.

Visitors from around the world visit our school because we have 84 nationalities of students.

We transitioned from being a junior high school to a middle school and are making significant progress.

Additional general comments included:

Our middle school is a success because teachers who did not want it could move to the high school and those who did received extensive staff development.

These transition years are very important.

We are working hard to implement the middle school philosophy and practices to the school and to develop positive attitudes.

There is a strong need for middle school teacher certification.

Eliminated interscholastic sports.

Anything is possible if you do not give up no matter what the odds.

The exemplary elements listed by respondents were positive and encouraging. Both the large number of schools responding to this open-ended survey item, and the rich responses, hold much promise for the present and future success of America's middle schools. The general comments made by respondents were diverse and reflected both the successes and frustrations of establishing and maintaining developmentally responsive schools for young adolescents. □

Part III

IN SUMMARY AND IN PERSPECTIVE

14.
CONCLUSIONS AND RECOMMENDATIONS

This chapter includes conclusions based primarily on the data collected in the 1968, 1988, and 1993 studies. Recommendations regarding the messages inherent in the data are also offered for consideration. These conclusions and recommendations are certainly not the only ones to be made based on this comprehensive study of America's middle schools. Readers are encouraged to explore the data and draw their own conclusions. The following discussion focuses on findings that seem especially important to the future success of middle schools.

The term "middle school" is used throughout this chapter, but is not intended to indicate that these findings are not important to junior high schools or schools with other grade organizations that include the middle level grades (e g , K-8 and 7-12). Indeed, results from this study hold many implications for any school that includes young adolescents among its clients.

This discussion is based on the premise that the weaknesses of middle school education should be acknowledged and frankly discussed and that successes should be recognized and celebrated. How else can the struggle to cast aside programs and practices that were designed for other developmental age groups be carried out? This study is also based on the premise that before significant long-term reform of middle level education can become a reality, we must indeed know where we are, how far we have come, where we should be headed, and how to get there. Results from this study will provide clear assistance in this difficult and crucial journey.

For the purposes of organization, and to make it easier for readers to turn back to more detailed information if they wish, the following discussion is presented in the same order and uses virtually the same titles as the previous chapters.

THE 1968, 1988, AND 1993 STUDIES

GRADE ORGANIZATION TRENDS

Too frequently in the past, especially in the 1960s and 1970s, decisions regarding which grades should be placed in middle schools were based on expediency rather on what was best for young adolescents. This practice led to some states having more than 25 different grade organizations which included one or more of the middle grades. Since many middle schools were not established to reform middle level education, it is not surprising that research studies conducted during the 1960s and 1970s found few differences between the middle schools and junior high schools of that period. Many of these schools simply changed their grade organization and retained the programs and practices of the traditional junior high school.

Despite the rationale for decisions made about grade organization patterns for the early middle schools, thousands of school districts did place grades 5-8 or 6-8 in middle schools. Fortunately, professional personnel at a significant number of these new middle schools recognized the importance of developing specialized developmentally responsive programs for young adolescents and pioneered exemplary practice which helped establish the middle school movement as a serious, national reform effort. These schools made significant contributions to the progress of middle school education by modeling successful practice.

Although some grade organization decisions continue to be made based on expediency, decisions about which grades should be included in middle schools established from the early 1980s to the present time have been made primarily on what is best for young adolescents. For example, the 1988 study found that the number one reason for establishing middle schools was "to provide a program designed for the age group."

However, the importance of which grades, and therefore, which developmental age groups, are placed in middle schools seems to have escaped some school districts as they continue to place young adolescents in elementary schools (K-8), high schools (7-12), and two-grade middle schools. (Two-grade middle schools cause young adolescents to make three transitions from one school to another in four years and separates young adolescents into multiple schools). While making these ill-informed decisions, statements such as "It is what happens in a school that is important, not which grade levels are present" are often repeated to mask the fact that the decisions are being made for expediency while the best interest of young adolescents is given low priority or completely ignored. Those believing that grade organization is not a key factor in the success levels of middle schools need only to reflect on the findings of this and other recent studies to see the fallacy of this assumption.

Conclusions

Increasing numbers of school districts across the nation are moving to a three-tier school organization which usually includes separately organized middle schools with grades 5-8, 6-8, or 7-8. Decisions regarding grade organization are increasingly being made based on what is best for young adolescents rather than on expediency and tradition.

Recommendations

Grade organization decisions should be driven by the developmental characteristics, needs, and interests of young adolescents rather than by expediency. Middle schools should house grades 5-8 or 6-8.

ENROLLMENT, ARTICULATION, AND DATES OF ESTABLISHMENT

SCHOOL ENROLLMENTS

As noted in Chapter 2, there is no research base that clearly demonstrates that one particular size student population is inherently better than another size student population. This does not mean, however, that the number of young adolescents attending a middle school is unimportant and should not come under scrutiny when decisions are being made about the sizes of student populations in middle schools. Too frequently it is automatically assumed that "small is better than large" or "bigger is better than small." Neither of these assumptions is necessarily accurate and the situation is compounded by the questions of "How small is small and how big is big?" It does seem, however, that middle schools can become so small that it is difficult to offer a full program (some schools in the current study had fewer than 100 students) or so big that there is an ever present danger of depersonalization (some schools in the current study had more than 2000 students).

It was encouraging to find that the percentage of middle schools with enrollments between 401 and 800 had remained rather constant over the

25 years considered in this study. However, the percentages of small middle schools (less than 401) had decreased and large middle schools (more than 800) increased. In the absence of definitive research identifying a specific middle school size as ideal, the authors agree with results from a 1992 study which found that middle school principals believed that between 400 and 599 is an optimum size for middle schools (Valentine, Clark, Irvin, Keefe, & Melton, 1993).

Conclusion
Overall, enrollments in middle schools are becoming larger.

Recommendations
When possible, the school populations of middle schools should be kept in the 400 to 800 student range. When schools must be very small or very large, care should be taken to organize them in ways that allow and promote developmentally responsive programs, (i.e., cross-grade team organization in small schools and school-within-a-school in large schools).

ARTICULATION

Articulation continues to be a vital part of the mission and operation of middle schools and is a major factor in determining success levels of those schools. Results from this study confirm that this mission is being taken seriously by today's middle schools, and significant progress has been made toward working closely with elementary and high schools to help young adolescents successfully make transitions into and out of middle schools. For example, 90% of 6-8 schools scheduled visitations for elementary students from feeder schools and 84% of middle schools reported obtaining data from feeder schools as well as providing it to high schools. Seven of the nine categories utilized in the survey showed increases from the earlier national surveys (Alexander, 1968; McEwin & Alexander, 1989). On a less encouraging note, a minority of schools reported visitations by middle school teachers to elementary or high schools.

Conclusion
Positive and continuing trends, as well as noteworthy accomplishments, have been made in the area of articulation.

Recommendations
Articulation remains a major mission of the middle school and should receive increased attention to assure that all young

adolescents are assisted in making smooth and meaningful transitions from elementary schools to middle schools as well as from middle schools to high schools. The focus of articulation should also be on assisting young adolescents in making successful transitions from childhood to adolescence.

DATES OF ESTABLISHMENT

Results from this study show a strong continuing trend in the establishment of separately organized middle schools. The popularity of grades 6-8 middle schools has continued to increase in recent years as evidenced by the fact that 29% of the randomly selected middle schools in the current study reported having been established since 1988 and 59% since 1980. Sixteen percent of 5-8 schools, 24% of 7-8 schools, and 17% of 7-9 schools reported establishment dates of 1988 or later.

Conclusion

A significant number of middle schools have been established in recent years.

Recommendations

Separately organized middle schools where professional personnel focus directly and exclusively on the needs, interests, and characteristics of young adolescents should continue to be established. Careful study should precede the decision about which grade levels and what size school populations to include in these newly established schools.

PREPARATION PRIOR TO OPENING MIDDLE SCHOOLS

Planning programs and practices for new middle schools is closely associated with the ultimate success of these schools. Data received regarding preparatory activities conducted before the middle schools in this study opened showed continued growth in preparatory activities when compared to the 1968 and 1988 studies. For example, the majority of 6-8 middle schools engaged in a year or more of faculty study and district planning prior to the original openings of the schools. Other common activities included visits to other middle schools, staff development efforts, and summer faculty workshops.

Conclusions

The use of preparatory activities prior to opening new middle schools has increased during the 25 years period considered by this study. However, some new middle schools engaged in very few preparatory activities prior to establishment.

Recommendations

Carefully planned preparatory activities should be conducted prior to opening new middle schools. These efforts should be inclusive of all stakeholders, utilize a wide range of activities, and continue well beyond the original opening of the new middle schools.

GRADE ORGANIZATION DECISIONS

Respondents were asked to indicate who was involved in the decisions regarding which grade levels should be included in their middle schools. As was the case in 1968 and 1988, the primary persons making these decisions continued to be system level administrators and principals. Some limited increase in the use of teachers in the decision making process was found.

Conclusion

The decisions regarding middle school grade organization were made primarily by system level administrators and building principals.

Recommendation

The individuals involved in middle school grade organization decisions should be expanded to include teachers, family members, and community groups.

MIDDLE SCHOOL INSTRUCTIONAL ORGANIZATION

CORE SUBJECT ORGANIZATIONAL PLANS

The use of interdisciplinary team organization in the core subjects of language arts, social studies, mathematics, and science has significantly increased in the 25 year period included in this study. As seen in Chapter 3, team organization is becoming the predominant organization plan for instruction in these subjects in the middle grades. Concurrently, the use of self-contained classrooms and departmentalization is declining in popularity.

Conclusion

The trend toward utilizing interdisciplinary team organization in the core subjects of language arts, social studies, mathematics, and science grew while the use of departmentalization and self-contained classrooms decreased.

Recommendation

All core subjects should be taught by interdisciplinary teams of teachers and the use of self-contained classrooms and departmentalization should be eliminated.

TEAM LEADER SELECTION

Methods for selecting team leaders were explored in the current study but not in the previous studies. This item was included to determine if certain methods were commonly used for this process. The following conclusions were drawn based on the data provided by respondents.

Conclusions

No single form of team leader selection emerged as dominant. The most popular form of selection of team leaders was by team members, followed by principal appointment. No team leader was present in 20% of schools using team organization.

Recommendation

All teams should have team leaders, and team members should have a major role in selecting those leaders.

HEALTH AND READING

Instructional plans for teaching health and reading were examined. The two most common patterns for health instruction varied by grade level. Health was most often incorporated with science at the sixth grade level with the second most popular plan being the separate subject approach. The pattern was reversed for grades seven and eight. Health was also integrated with physical education in a small number of middle schools.

Conclusions

The two most frequently utilized organizational plans for health instruction were separate subject and integrated with

*science. About 15% of middle schools taught health with physi-
cal education. It is not known which plan is most effective.*

Recommendation
*Whatever the instructional plan, health should be a high pri-
ority in middle school curriculum and instruction.*

Reading organized as a separate subject with its own period was the
most popular instructional plan at all grade levels. However, use of this
plan decreased in grades seven and eight. This trend was mirrored in the
increase of integrating reading with other content areas and/or the total
school program.

Conclusion
*Although the primary organizational plan for reading instruc-
tion was the separate subject plan, its use decreased both as a
separate subject within its own period and when blocked with
other content areas in the higher middle grades.*

Recommendation
*Reading should continue to be a high priority in the entire
middle grades instructional program.*

TEACHER PLANNING PERIODS

With increases in the use of interdisciplinary team organization in
middle schools, the importance of teachers having two planning periods
– one for individual planning and one for team planning – has been acknowledged in the literature. This study investigated the number of planning periods team members had.

Conclusions
*The majority of teachers in the total study worked in schools
where all teachers had one planning period. When compared
to other grade organizations in the current study, most or all
teachers in grades 6-8 middle schools had two planning periods (36%). Thirty-two percent of all schools in the study and
70% of 6-8 middle schools that utilized team organization provided most or all teachers with two planning periods.*

Recommendation
*All teachers teaching on teams should have two daily plan-
ning periods.*

REMEDIAL ARRANGEMENTS

Middle schools provide a range of remedial instructional arrangements for young adolescents. The three most popular remedial arrangements in grades 5-8, 6-8, and 7-8 middle schools were: (a) before and after school classes/coaching sessions; (b) summer school; and, (c) extra work/homework provided by the teacher. Grades 5-8 schools were most likely overall to have remedial arrangements and the 7-9 junior high least likely to do so.

Conclusions

The middle level schools in this study, with the exception of junior high schools, were engaged in a wide variety of remedial activities. The most popular remedial activities included before and after school classes, summer school, extra work provided by teachers, and pullout programs.

Recommendation

All middle level schools should conduct a wide range of remedial activities and programs and these remedial efforts should be given high priority.

SCHEDULING PLANS

The importance of flexible scheduling plans for middle schools is widely accepted. The current study explored the types of scheduling plans used by middle schools and compared the results with data from the 1988 study.

Conclusions

The dominant scheduling pattern was daily periods, uniform in length. However, a significant increase in the use of flexible scheduling and a decrease in self-contained classrooms had occurred since the 1988 study.

Recommendation

All middle schools should implement flexible scheduling so that developmentally responsive curriculum and instruction can occur.

CURRICULUM

BASIC SUBJECTS TAKEN ALL YEAR BY ALL STUDENTS

An overwhelming percentage of 6-8 middle schools reported that all students at their schools took the basic subjects for the entire year. This result mirrored data obtained in the 1988 study and is evidence of the continued emphasis placed on the basic subjects in middle schools. Language arts and mathematics were the most frequently required year-long subjects (99%). Physical education was also included in this section because of its importance at the middle level. Unfortunately, the percentages of schools providing physical education to all students for the entire school year had decreased since the 1988 study.

Conclusions

The basic subjects of social studies, language arts, science, and mathematics are major emphases in the nation's middle schools. In the overwhelming majority of all middle schools, students take these subjects for the entire school year. However, the year-long offering of physical education had decreased since the 1988 study.

Recommendations

The basic subjects of science, language arts, mathematics, and social studies should continue to receive strong emphasis in middle schools. All students should take physical education for the entire school year.

REQUIRED AND ELECTIVE COURSES

Middle level schools offered a wide range of both required and elective course offerings. Several course offerings at the sixth grade level showed significant gains (e.g., health, computers, sex education) from the 1988 study while others experienced decreases (e.g., reading, art, general music, home economics, industrial arts). The most frequently offered courses at the seventh grade level were band, chorus, art, orchestra, foreign language, industrial arts, home economics, and computers. Of these courses, none had decreased in usage since the 1988 study (there were no 1988 data on some course offerings). Eighth grade students were most often offered band, chorus, art, foreign language, industrial arts, home economics, computers, and orchestra. Courses in home economics and industrial arts had decreased slightly since the 1988 study.

Conclusions

Particular patterns of various courses as required and elective developed in the five-year period between the 1988 and 1993 studies. Subjects such as art, computers, foreign language, and sex education, when available as electives, increased. Health and foreign language exhibited the same pattern when offered as required subjects, while usage of reading as a required course decreased during the same time period. Similar patterns were found for all grade organizations included in the 1988 and 1993 studies.

Recommendations

A rich variety of elective and required courses should continue to be part of the middle school curriculum and these courses should be carefully monitored to assure inclusion of all students. Decisions on course offerings should be made based on the developmental characteristics, needs, and interests of young adolescents.

LENGTH OF TIME FOR SELECTED COURSES

Course lengths for required and elective courses at the seventh grade level were investigated with the choices being a full year, one-half year, or less than one-half year. Large-group performance courses and reading were most often offered for the entire year. Less-than-half time courses typically included traditional elective offerings such as industrial arts and careers as well as some relatively new courses such as sex education and computers. A relatively small percentage of middle schools offered semester long courses.

Conclusions

The length of required and elective seventh grade courses are typically year-long or less than one-half year. The semester-long plan is used at the seventh grade level in only about one-third of middle schools.

Recommendation

The length of time allocated for required and elective courses at all grade levels should be based on the overall needs of all young adolescents, not just those participating in selected courses/activities and these decisions regarding the use of that time should be thoughtful and reflect the developmental realities of young adolescents.

SELECTED STUDENT ACTIVITIES

Student activities were included in the study to gain a more complete understanding of curricular offerings. Student councils were the most frequently offered activities and were more common than was the case in the 1988 study. Publications, honor societies, and social dancing showed significant gains in popularity.

Conclusions

Traditional student activities such as publications, honor societies, and social dancing increased over the 25 year period included in this study. More activities were offered to seventh and eighth grade students and fewer to fifth and sixth grade students.

Recommendation

Student activities as part of the middle school curriculum should be carefully selected and implemented, and should be diverse enough to allow and encourage wide participation of all young adolescents.

INTEREST/MINI COURSE PROGRAMS

Information regarding the offering of short-term, student interest-centered courses revealed that 5-8 and 6-8 schools were much more likely to offer such courses that were 7-8 or 7-9 schools. These courses were most often offered daily, followed by one and two days per week. The most popular length of time provided for these courses was either 4 to 6 or 7 to 9 weeks. These courses tended to be scheduled for longer numbers of weeks in 7-9 junior high schools.

Conclusions

Approximately one-third of 5-8 and 6-8 schools, and one fourth of 7-8 and 7-9 schools had interest class/mini-course programs. These classes generally lasted about six to nine weeks and met on a daily basis.

Recommendation

Rich and varied interest class/mini-courses should be implemented in all middle schools.

INSTRUCTION AND REPORTING PUPIL PROGRESS

ESTIMATES OF IMPLEMENTATION LEVELS OF INTERDISCIPLINARY INSTRUCTION

The majority of respondents estimated that interdisciplinary instruction was practiced at their school about 1-20% of the time. The percentages of schools using interdisciplinary instruction more than 20% of the time decreased dramatically. Overall, about one-fourth of the schools in the study estimated that from 21-40% of instructional time was interdisciplinary in nature. Sixteen percent of respondents estimated that their schools used interdisciplinary instruction more than 40% of the time.

Conclusions

Although it is encouraging that interdisciplinary instruction is being practiced in the majority of schools in the study, it has not yet become institutionalized into common practice. Interdisciplinary instruction is still something that is done "occasionally" rather than "regularly."

Recommendation

Major efforts should be made to implement interdisciplinary curriculum and instruction on a regular basis in all middle schools.

USE OF SELECTED INSTRUCTIONAL STRATEGIES

Inquiry into how frequently selected instructional strategies were used in middle schools revealed that middle schools employed direct instruction at very high levels of implementation. For example, about 90% of 6-8 schools regularly taught using direct instruction. The reluctance to move away from this method is alarming when its ineffectiveness is considered. Cooperative learning was used by about one-half of the schools and approximately one-third reported utilizing inquiry-teaching. About one-half of the middle schools used independent study as an instructional method.

Conclusions

The predominate instructional methodology used in middle schools was direct instruction. Cooperative learning, inquiry-teaching, and independent study were utilized in smaller percentages of schools.

Recommendation

Middle schools should make immediate and sustained efforts to dramatically alter the use of direct instruction as the primary means of teaching young adolescents and move toward more developmentally responsive instructional methodologies.

PUPIL PROGRESS REPORTING

Many methods of reporting pupil progress to students, family members, and teachers were reported by schools in this study. Although the use of letter scales had declined somewhat during the 25 years considered in this study, it was still the most popular means of reporting pupil progress. The second most used method was parent conferences, followed by informal written notes. These two methods experienced significant increases between the 1968 and 1988 studies, but declined in use between 1988 and 1993. A noticeable decline in the use of other methods of reporting pupil progress reporting had also occurred. The satisfactory-unsatisfactory scale was used by about one-third of schools, an increase since the earlier studies. The use of word scales also increased in the 25 year period. The use of portfolios for reporting pupil progress was not investigated in the 1968 and 1988 studies. However, 22% of schools in the 1993 study reported they used this new method.

Conclusions

The use of word scales, satisfactory-unsatisfactory, informal written notes, and parent conferences has increased over the 25 year period. However, the most popular method of reporting pupil progress was the letter scale.

Recommendation

Middle schools should use a variety of methods to report pupil progress to parents and others and this reporting should be individual and positive in nature.

INSTRUCTIONAL GROUPING PRACTICES

CRITERIA FOR GROUPING STUDENTS FOR BASIC SUBJECTS

Respondents were asked to indicate which criteria were used for student grouping for instruction in the basic subjects of language arts, social studies, science, and mathematics. The six criteria examined were: (a) achievement tests; (b) I.Q. tests; (c) teacher recommendation; (d) parental input; (e) previous academic records; and, (f) random assignment. Results from the current study revealed a decrease in the use of all of these criteria except random assignment. (No previous data were available on parental input).

Results from the current study found that the most popular criteria used for grouping were teacher recommendations, previous academic records, and random assignment. Between 1988 and 1993, the use of random grouping increased significantly at all grade levels (e.g., sixth grade, 25% in 1988; 52% in 1993). This trend away from tracking and movement toward grouping young adolescents randomly for instruction in the basic subjects is indeed encouraging.

Conclusions

Random grouping is growing significantly in popularity at middle schools. The use of all other criteria used for grouping students for instruction in the basic subjects had decreased.

Recommendations

The practice of grouping young adolescents randomly for basics instruction should increase until it becomes universal practice. Accompanying this abandonment of tracking must be a commitment to more effective methods of grouping young adolescents for instruction.

CRITERIA FOR GROUPING STUDENTS FOR ELECTIVE SUBJECTS

The same criteria were used to investigate grouping students for elective subjects. The four most popular criteria were random assignment, previous academic record, parental input, and teacher recommendation. Random grouping was the most frequently utilized criterion and was used by the majority of schools. Random instructional grouping was used most frequently by 5-8 schools (38%), followed by 7-8 schools (36%), and 6-8 schools (32%). Grades 7-9 junior high schools were the least likely grade organization to utilize random grouping (20%). Over-all, about one-third of all schools in the study grouped students ran-domly for elective subjects.

Conclusion
Random grouping was the most popular criterion for group-ing young adolescents for elective subjects.

Recommendations
Random grouping should continue to be the primary crite-rion for grouping young adolescents for elective courses. Care should be taken to assure that all students have opportunities to participate in this important part of the middle school cur-riculum.

GROUPING PRACTICES FOR TEACHER-BASED GUIDANCE

Random grouping was the most often used criterion for grouping stu-dents for teacher-based guidance programs. All other criteria for group-ing students for teacher-based guidance programs declined over the 25 year time span considered in this study.

Conclusion
Random grouping is the primary criterion for grouping stu-dents for teacher-based guidance programs.

Recommendations
Random grouping should be the major criterion used for making decisions regarding placement of young adolescents into advisory groups. Although special circumstances will at times make teacher recommendations appropriate, great care should be taken not to group students for teacher-based guid-ance programs based on additional criteria, such as tracking decisions made for subject assignments or to make scheduling classes in the performing arts easier.

OPERATING POLICIES REGARDING ABILITY GROUPING

Three major policies emerged in exploring results from investigation of operating policies concerning ability grouping: (a) grouping at all grade levels in certain subjects; (b) grouping at certain grade levels but not in all subjects; and, (c) random grouping. Two additional practices that were seldom reported were grouping at all levels in all subjects, and grouping at certain grade levels in all subjects.

Twenty-four percent of all schools in the total study reported grouping in certain grade levels but not in all subjects. As previously noted, random grouping was used by about one-third of all schools in the study. The 7-9 junior high school was most likely to ability group at all grade levels in certain subjects and least likely to use random grouping. The 5-8 school was most likely to use random grouping and grouping at certain grade levels but not in all subjects, but least likely to use ability grouping at all grade levels in certain subjects. The 7-8 school was least likely to use ability grouping at certain grade levels but not all subjects.

Conclusions

For all schools included in the study, the most frequently utilized operating policy for grouping students was grouping at all grade levels in certain subjects (37%). This was followed by random grouping (32%), and grouping at certain grade levels but not in all subjects (24%).

Recommendations

Operating policies for grouping students should focus on the inclusion of all students and be based upon the assumption that all students are capable of learning and have the right to do so. For the great majority of time, students should be grouped and regrouped in flexible ways within classes and/ or teams.

TEACHER-BASED GUIDANCE PROGRAMS

The percentages of middle schools with teacher-based guidance programs, with the exception of 7-9 junior high schools, increased between the 1988 and 1993 studies. The most prevalent pattern for frequency of advisory meetings was daily. However, this practice of daily meetings decreased somewhat in all grade organizations from the 1988 to the 1993 studies. There was also a significant decrease in the percentages of schools that used an "administrative homeroom" time frame of 15 minutes or less. Along with the decline of abbreviated advisory periods, there was a significant increase in the percentages of schools that scheduled 16-30 minute meetings (65%). Use of the 31-45 minute time frame also increased. Overall, 80% of all school organizations with advisory periods schedule them for between 16 and 45 minutes. Grades 6-8 schools were twice as likely to schedule more than 20 minutes per meeting than other grade organizations in the study.

Advisory programs are generally staffed by classroom teachers. However, some schools also use administrators and support staff. Grades 6-8 schools most frequently reported using the total staff as advisors. The most commonly used groups, other than classroom teachers, were resource teachers, counselors, and administrators.

Conclusions

The use of teacher-based guidance programs has increased significantly during the 25 years considered in this study. This increase occurred in all grade organizations in the current study except 7-9 junior high schools. The majority of all 6-8 schools had implemented this essential middle school component. Most schools with teacher-based guidance programs scheduled them to meet daily. Classroom teachers were the primary group that staffed these meetings, but in many schools other professional staff members were also included.

Recommendations

Carefully planned teacher-based guidance programs should be a part of all middle schools. Advisory groups should meet daily for at least 25 minutes with virtually all professional personnel having an advisory group. The curriculum for these programs should be carefully planned and the programs given top priority by the total professional staff.

INTRAMURAL AND INTERSCHOLASTIC SPORTS

INTRAMURAL SPORTS

It is widely accepted in the literature that intramural sports programs are an important component of effective middle schools. However, after significant increases in percentages of schools with intramural programs occurred between the 1968 and 1988 studies, percentages of 5-8 and 6-8 middle schools with such programs declined between 1988 and 1993. Intramural sports programs remained at about the same level of implementation at 7-8 and 7-9 schools during this five-year period.

Conclusion

When results from the current study were considered, the use of intramural sports programs decreased during the period from 1988 to 1993.

Recommendations

All middle schools should have strong, effective, developmentally responsive, and inclusive intramural sports programs that involve the large majority of young adolescents at those schools and these programs should receive the attention and efforts needed to make them highly effective and developmentally responsive. Intramural programs should have a higher priority than interscholastic sports programs.

INTERSCHOLASTIC SPORTS PROGRAMS

The percentages of 6-8 middle schools reporting interscholastic sports programs at the seventh grade level increased between 1988 and 1993 while little change occurred at the eighth grade level. During this same time period sixth grade interscholastic sports programs decreased slightly (4%). The percentages of interscholastic sports programs for seventh grade in 5-8 schools decreased from 1988 to 1993 and increased in 7-8 schools.

Fifteen percent of all schools reported that interscholastic sports had been eliminated from their programs. Of those schools adding sports to their interscholastic programs, soccer and volleyball were most often listed as the new sports. Schools eliminating one or more sports from their programs most often dropped football, the most violent and dangerous sport included in middle school interscholastic sports programs.

Conclusions

Approximately 25% of schools in the total study provided interscholastic sports programs at the sixth grade level, 77% for seventh graders, and 79% for eighth graders. Increasing percentages of middle schools had interscholastic programs for seventh and eighth graders.

Recommendations

When interscholastic programs are offered at the middle school level, great care should be taken to carefully select which sports are to be included and which age groups are permitted to participate. These sports programs should be offered only if

> *qualified coaches are available who are knowledgeable about early adolescence and are willing to put students' best interest ahead of the desire to win games. Interscholastic programs at all middle schools should undergo a comprehensive study which examines their developmental appropriateness. Results of these studies should be used to determine the nature of interscholastic sports programs.*

FACULTY

Sixty-two percent of respondents estimated that less than 25% of teachers at their schools had specialized middle level professional preparation. Changes in faculties with specialized professional preparation beyond the 25% level between 1988 and 1993 were small except at the 7-9 junior high school level where substantial declines were found. There was a 2% increase in schools where it was estimated that 25%-50% of teachers had received specialized middle level professional preparation. The percentages of schools where it was estimated that 76%-100% of faculty members had received specialized preparation increased by only 1% between the 1988 and 1993 studies.

Conclusions
The largest block of faculties with specialized middle school preparation was less than 25%. This figure remained constant from 1988 to 1993.

Recommendations
Progress toward reaching the point where all young adolescents are taught by teachers who have acquired the specialized knowledge, skills, and dispositions needed to be highly successful has been extremely slow. As long as teachers without the specialized knowledge, skills, and dispositions needed to be highly successful are permitted to teach young adolescents, only modest progress in making all middle schools developmentally responsive will be made. Therefore, collaborative efforts should be initiated to enact mandatory middle level teacher licensure requirements that encourage and require teacher preparation institutions to design and implement programs specifically designed for prospective and practicing middle level teachers. Quality teacher preparation programs which provide specialized professional preparation for pro-

spective and practicing middle school teachers should be widely available in all states.

SCHOOL EVALUATION

Respondents to the 1968 study reported that standardized tests, follow-up studies, accrediting evaluations, and self-studies were popular means of school evaluation. The 1988 respondents included these school evaluation methods, but also reported measures such as: (a) annual end-of-year evaluations by parents, students, and faculty; (b) periodic evaluations using state-developed and/or other models; (c) task forces, councils, committees of parents, teachers, administrators and others; and, (d) student, staff, and parent polls.

Analysis of the open-ended responses regarding school evaluation in the current study revealed a wide range of school evaluation measures used by responding schools. Many were traditional measures of student outcomes such as scores on standardized achievement tests, state mandated procedures, and regional accrediting associations' evaluations. However, other forms of school evaluation that were innovative and less traditional were also reported (e.g., use of *Turning Points* recommendations and the National School Recognition application). National standards and recommendations, regional accreditation associations and standards, state evaluation procedures, district evaluation procedures, and school evaluation procedures were among the most frequently reported evaluation plans.

Conclusions

Results from the current survey regarding school evaluation compare favorably with results from the 1968 and 1988 surveys. An expansion of evaluation methods occurred. The richness and variety of school evaluation plans provided by respondents to the current study indicate a trend toward including both traditional and innovative school evaluation procedures.

Recommendations

Middle schools should use a wide range of school evaluation plans and procedures that include, but move beyond, traditional forms. Wide involvement of many stakeholders should be sought; the school evaluation process should be continuous rather than being limited to periodic formal activities.

Respondents were asked to list problems experienced in becoming effective middle schools. The problems most frequently listed in the 1968 study were teacher adjustment, finances, and excessive student populations. Results of the 1988 study included many of the same problems encountered by schools responding to the 1968 study. However, additional problems such as flexible scheduling and interscholastic sports programs were also frequently listed.

Problems reported in the current study included systemic problems that are encountered in schools with many different grade organizations (K-8, 9-12) and middle school specific problems such as teacher-based guidance programs, interdisciplinary teams and instruction, and intramural sports programs. These kinds of problems were typical in schools with all grade organizations included in the current study.

Staff was the most frequently listed problem by respondents in the current study. These problems were often encountered because of the lack of specialized knowledge about teaching young adolescents in middle schools (see Chapter 12 for additional reasons). Lack of adequate funding was also frequently considered a problem. Additional problems given involved students in school settings (e.g., motivating and involving students and providing for students who were below grade level expectations) and family-member related concerns such as lack of parental care for some students.

The two broad categories of programmatic problems that emerged were school wide concerns (e.g., struggling with homogeneous vs. heterogeneous grouping and scheduling students for a variety of classes and programs) and middle level focused problems (teacher-based guidance and interscholastic sports programs). Respondents also identified a variety of problems associated with family members and the local communities (e.g., community opposition to teacher-based guidance and lack of family/community involvement).

Problems encountered at the district and state levels included restrictive state guidelines and mandated state and district policies that dictated schedules. However, throughout this section the recurring theme was the lack of knowledge and/or support for middle level education at the district level by superintendents, central office staff, and boards of education. There were some middle schools in the study that reported that no significant problems had occurred in establishing and maintaining their programs.

Conclusions

The kinds of problems identified by respondents over the 25 years considered in this study revealed some that have been present since the beginning of the middle school movement and contributed to the failures of the junior high school (i.e., the lack of specialized teacher preparation). Problems that emerged for the first time in the current study reflect the changing nature of this nation and its schools. As decision makers at middle schools attempt to transform their traditional schools into places where all young adolescents are highly valued and where there is an expectation that all students can and will learn, problems such as those identified here are to be expected. It is important to identify these problems so that solutions can be sought that make transformations possible.

Recommendations

Stakeholders who make crucial decisions that determine the course of individual middle schools should explore pioneering middle schools that are already highly successful. By examining the knowledge base of successful practice and becoming knowledgeable about middle school research, sound decisions will emerge that will lead to highly successful middle schools.

EXEMPLARY ELEMENTS

It is encouraging to find that 70% of respondents listed one or more elements they considered exemplary. It is also encouraging to note that the most frequently listed category was "teachers." This, in combination with the response that resistance from teachers was the most frequently encountered problem, points to the importance of the roles teachers play in determining the successes and failures of middle schools and the young adolescents who attend them.

The core subjects (mathematics, social studies, language arts, and science) were the second most frequently listed exemplary element. This indicates that the core subjects continue to be highly regarded and are considered a major responsibility of middle schools. Teaming and teacher-based guidance, two essential elements of successful middle schools, and family members/community involvement completed the five most popular exemplary elements.

The next five most often listed exemplary elements included the use of computers and other technology, supportive climate/caring environment, the arts, exploratory/elective courses, and scheduling. These responses are very positive since they reflect key elements of developmentally responsive programs. They also point out that although the basic subjects are a major part of the middle school curriculum, the exploratory subjects and the arts are also highly regarded and included as important components of the middle school curriculum. The inclusion of caring and supportive environments is encouraging and the recognition of the importance of technology in instruction indicates an understanding of how its proper use enhances learning.

Positive directions toward effective middle schools were also evident in the next five choices. These were test scores, exceptional children's programs, the instructional programs, students, and at-risk programs. The number of middle schools reporting exemplary standardized test scores help inform the public about the academic success of young adolescents. Middle schools are not only working hard to establish and maintain programs for exceptional children and at-risk students, but consider those programs highly successful. It is also gratifying that many schools listed their students as exemplary elements. This seems especially significant since this survey item used the very generic term "elements" and did not list possible choices.

The final five of the most frequently listed elements included intramural sports programs, student recognition programs, student activities, discipline, and curriculum. All these, and the remaining exemplary elements (described in Chapter 13) represent very positive directions for middle schools.

Readers should understand that respondents were not asked to prioritize their exemplary elements if they listed more than one. Neither were the categories used to analyze the data included in the survey. In fact there are more than 1000 responses not included in the top 20 most often listed responses. These responses, summarized in Chapter 13, are rich and worthy of exploration.

Conclusions

The 20 most frequently listed exemplary elements, and the more than 1000 additional responses listed by respondents, are encouraging for the future of middle level education. They are rich in variety and demonstrate the many successes accomplished by the courageous educators in our nation's middle schools who understand the importance of developmentally responsive programs and have taken actions based on that knowledge.

Recommendations

There should be planned efforts among middle schools to share their success with other schools and to learn from others. Lessons can be learned from individual schools, school districts, and other stakeholders about the keys to establishing, maintaining, and continually improving middle schools. □

15.
THE MIDDLE SCHOOL: FAD, FANTASY, OR REALITY

> **fad**: a practice or interest followed for a time with exaggerated zeal.
>
> **fantasy**: hallucination; a fanciful design or invention; the free play of creative imagination.
>
> **reality**: the quality or state of being real; a real event, entity, or state of affairs; the totality of real things and events.
>
> (*Merriam Webster's Collegiate Dictionary*, 1993)

I s the American middle school a fad that will be followed with exaggerated zeal and then abandoned as have many other past attempts to improve the educational opportunities of our nation's children? Is the concept of establishing separately organized, developmentally responsive schools that reflect what is known about the unique needs, characteristics, and interests of young adolescents only a hallucination? Are the many thousands of middle schools that now exist destined to be schools that are based more on rhetoric than reality?

Are middle schools pioneering a successful nationwide reform movement that will not only improve the education of young adolescents, but influence future directions of the tradition-bound American high school? Is it a fantasy to believe that at some future time middle schools will be staffed with teachers and other professional personnel who have received the specialized professional preparation necessary to be highly successful in teaching young adolescents? Will the traditional subject-centered curriculum that is so far removed from the real world – delivered primarily by the lecture and recitation mode – give way to a more meaningful integrated curriculum which will be taught in developmentally responsive ways?

ANSWERS OFFER MIXED RESULTS

The answers to these and related questions cannot yet be fully formulated. However, after analyzing the data from this comprehensive study, the authors have concluded that the success of the middle school movement at this point is significant but limited, and is, at the same time, both encouraging and discouraging. It is encouraging to see significant trends in programs and practices moving in directions that reflect developmental responsiveness, yet disappointing to learn that many middle schools continue to avoid changes in their school's environments that are so desperately needed.

Results from this study documented increasing numbers of middle schools utilizing developmentally sound practices and programs such as interdisciplinary team organization and teacher-based guidance. Additionally, the progress that has been made by the pioneers of the middle school movement in conceptualizing and establishing middle schools as institutions designed specifically and exclusively for the education of young adolescents is significant. This grassroots reform movement, which emerged primarily from individual schools and school districts, has been able to transform thousands of junior high schools into middle schools as well as influence large numbers of school districts with two-tier organizations to create three-tier ones that recognize the importance of the developmental stage of early adolescence. It has also led to the creation and development of growing numbers of model middle schools which are now spread across the nation. These and related accomplishments were guided by the work of middle school leaders such as William M. Alexander, Donald H. Eichhorn, and Paul George.

Unfortunately, however, the data also clearly showed that significant numbers of middle schools continue to follow unsuccessful and inappropriate practices such as departmentalization, rigid scheduling, and tracking, while failing to implement programs such as interdisciplinary team organization, flexible scheduling, and interdisciplinary instruction. These middle schools not only hurt the young adolescents who attend them, but cast shadows of doubt about the authenticity and legitimacy of the middle school movement itself.

DIRECTIONS NEEDED FOR PROGRESS

The directions to fully attain the goals of middle school education are known, and in most cases have been known about for years. Decisions made about middle school programs and practices should be based on successful middle school practices and programs. With growing numbers of model middle schools, why has progress been so slow and uneven? The answer is both very complex and amazingly simple. The roadblocks to success have been identified so targeting achievable goals is rather simple. Removing these roadblocks, however, is a complex process that will require collaborative efforts unparalleled in the history of middle level education.

Some selected examples of the "realities" that will help determine future directions traveled by the middle school movement are presented below. Reflecting on these points may contribute to a deeper understanding of the current status of middle school education and help determine priorities for future directions.

Characteristics, Needs, and Interests of Young Adolescents. A continuing difficulty in providing developmentally responsive schools for young adolescents is widespread ignorance about the characteristics, needs, and interests of the age group. Many people, both inside and outside the profession, are not only unenlightened about the age group, but hold negative stereotypes about them. They are often completely unaware of the lifelong influence of experiences youth undergo during these years when their values and attitudes are being formed.

Comprehensive efforts must be made to educate the profession and the public about the uniqueness of young adolescents so that their nature and potential can be understood, appreciated, and celebrated. Only when this barrier is removed will middle schools become fully functional, and what is more important, will their clients reach their full potential.

Developmentally Responsive Curriculum and Instruction. An additional difficulty faced by the middle school movement, which is directly linked to the developmental reality just discussed, is that large numbers of educators, policy-makers, family and community members, members of boards of education, and other stakeholders do not have accurate understandings of the nature of developmentally responsive curriculum, instruction, programs, or practices. Obviously, this lack of understanding frequently leads to decisions that are counterproductive to successful middle level schooling. Steps must be taken to spread the knowledge about the kinds of schooling needed by young adolescents and to inform all concerned about the success of schools that have already implemented exemplary programs.

Specialized Middle Level Professional Preparation. One of the major reasons for the limited success of junior high schools was the lack of specialized professional preparation programs for junior high school teachers and other professional personnel. This problem has not been remedied in many states with the result being that almost anyone with a teaching license of any kind is considered qualified to teach young adolescents. This means that the majority of all middle level teachers begin their careers without having had opportunities to attain the specialized knowledge, skills, and dispositions needed to be highly successful teachers of young adolescents. This lack of specialized professional preparation has many serious implications for the success of the middle school movement. For example, teachers and other professional personnel with limited knowledge about the nature of developmentally responsive middle school curriculum, instruction, and schooling often resist programs and practices needed by their students. Staffing middle school classrooms and schools with teachers and other professionals who do not have specialized professional preparation diminishes the chances that middle schools will be highly successful.

IS THE MIDDLE SCHOOL FAD, FANTASY, OR REALITY?

Middle schools are certainly not a fad, for fads are short-lived and do not develop and prosper for three decades or more. The real question may be: Will middle schools live up to their promise by serving young adolescents in developmentally responsive ways? The answer to this question has not yet been fully answered on a national basis. However, in some schools and communities the answer is *yes*.

Middle schools are also not fantasies, for it has been demonstrated that they can be successful in all types of communities and serve well the diverse young adolescents of our nation. In schools and school districts where the reality of establishing these schools is a fantasy, it remains such because of the actions, or inactions, of those responsible for educational decisions. In these situations, the fantasy can become reality if those responsible work hard enough and long enough at the correct tasks.

Indeed middle schools are a reality. There are currently more than 12,000 middle level schools in the nation and the vast majority of all young adolescents attend these schools. Their quality and degree of developmental responsiveness vary from place to place, but their existence gives promise to the possibility that some day all young adolescents will have the kinds of schooling they need and deserve.

WHAT ABOUT THE FUTURE?

The future of middle school education is in the hands of those who now make the decisions about which priorities will be followed. The substantial progress achieved to this point will only be sustained, and new goals achieved, if all involved take critical stances and act upon their specialized knowledge, experience, and dispositions. Collaborative actions that go beyond simple cooperation are required because it is clear that the middle school movement will not be fully successful until the assistance of those outside the school understand and support the goals and objectives of the middle school concept.

In summary, much has been achieved during the middle school movement, yet much remains to be accomplished. It is crucial that all pretenses be stripped away, that excuses for lack of progress be eliminated, and that realities be faced with the courage and determination needed to win the battle for exemplary middle schools for the young adolescents of our great nation. In many ways, this battle will be won or lost on a school-by-school, district-by-district basis. This should not be discouraging, however, for it means that each person has an important role to play, and that role profoundly and directly affects the lives of young adolescents. What professional opportunity could be more meaningful?

Will the American middle school reach the potential that is described in its goals and objectives? Will the dedicated work of middle level professionals and other stakeholders result in rich, positive learning environments for young adolescents? Does the middle school movement have the potential to profoundly change the education of young adolescents in significant and powerful ways? The authors are cautiously optimistic that the answers are *yes*.□

References

Alexander, W. M. (1968). *A survey of organizational patterns of reorganized middle schools.* Washington, D.C.: United States Department of Health, Education, and Welfare.

Alexander, W. M. (1995). The junior high school: A changing view. In G. Hass & K. Wiles (Eds.), *Readings in Curriculum* (pp. 418-425). Boston: Allyn and Bacon. Reprinted in *Middle School Journal, 26*(3), 21-24.

Alexander, W. M., Williams, E. L., Compton, M., Hines, V. A., Prescott, D., & Kealy, R. (1969). *The emergent middle school,* (2nd ed.). New York: Holt, Rinehart and Winston.

Alexander. W. M., & McEwin, C. K. (1989a). *Earmarks of schools in the middle: A research report.* Boone, NC: Appalachian State University. (ERIC Document Reproduction Service No. ED 312 312)

Alexander. W. M., & McEwin, C. K. (1989b). *Schools in the middle: Status and progress,* Columbus, OH: National Middle School Association.

Beane, J. A., (1993). *A middle school curriculum: From rhetoric to reality.* Columbus, OH: National Middle School Association.

Beneditto, W. (1990, December 10). Pro career just a dream for most kids. *USA Today*, 13A.

Brooks, K., & Edwards, F. (1978). *The middle school in transition: A research report on the status of the middle school movement.* Lexington, KY: The Center for Professional Development, University of Kentucky.

Carnegie Council on Adolescent Development (1989). *Turning points: Preparing American youth for the 21st Century.* New York: Carnegie Corporation of New York.

Cawelti, G. (1988, November). Middle schools a better match with early adolescent needs, ASCD survey finds. *ASCD Curriculum Update,* 1-12.

Compton, M. F. (1976). The middle school: A status report. *Middle School Journal, 7*(2), 3-5.

Dryfoos, J. G. (1990). *Adolescents at risk: Prevalence and prevention.* New York: Oxford University Press.

Educational Research Service (1969). *Middle schools in action.* Washington, D.C.: American Association of School Administrators and Research Division of National Education Association.

Erb, T. O., & Doda, N. M. (1989). *Team organization: Promise — Practices and possibilities.* Washington, D.C.: National Education Association.

Epstein, J. L., & Mac Iver, D. J. (1990). *Education in the middle grades: National practices and trends.* Columbus, OH: National Middle School Association.

Findlay, S. (1987, October 5). Breaks of the game, *U. S. News and World Report*, 75-77.

George, P. S. (1991). Student development and middle level school organization: A prolegomenon, *Midpoints, 1*(1), 1-12.

George, P. S., & Alexander, W. M. (1993). *The exemplary middle school* (2nd. ed). New York: Harcourt Brace Jovanovich.

Gruhn, W. T., & Douglass, H. R. (1947). *The modern junior high school.* New York: The Ronald Press.

Hechinger, F. M. (1992). *Fateful choices: Healthy youth for the 21st Century.* New York: Hill and Wang.

Kohn, A. (1986). Is competition more enjoyable? On sports, play and fun. In A. Kohn, *No contest: The case against competition* (pp. 79-95). Boston: Houghton Mifflin.

McEwin, C. K. (1994). Interscholastic sports and young adolescents. *Transescence: The Journal on Emerging Adolescent Education, 22*(1), 21-28.

McEwin, C. K., & Clay, R. M. (1983). *Middle level education in the United States: A national comparative study of practices and programs of middle and junior high schools.* Boone, NC: Appalachian State University.

McEwin, C. K., & Dickinson, T. S. (1995). *The professional preparation of middle level teachers: Profiles of successful programs.* Columbus, OH: National Middle School Association.

Mellinger, M., & Rackauskas, J. A. (1970). *Quest for identity: National survey of the middle school – 1969-70.* Chicago: Chicago State College.

Merriam Webster's collegiate dictionary (10th ed.). (1993). Springfield, MA: Merriam Webster.

Micheli, L. J. (1980, April/June). Etiological assessment of overuse stress factors in athletes. *Nova Scotia Medical Bulletin*, 43-47.

Micheli, L. J. (1990, October, 29). Children and sports, *Newsweek*, 12.

National Commission on the Role of the School and the Community in Improving Adolescent Health (1990). *Code Blue: Uniting for healthier youth*. Washington, D.C.: American Medical Association and the National Association of States Boards of Education.

New York State Department of Education. (1989). *Regents policy statement on middle-level education and schools with middle-level grades*. Albany, NY: Author.

Scales, P. C. (1992). *Windows of opportunity: Improving middle grades teacher preparation*. Carrboro, NC: Center for Early Adolescence.

Scales, P. C., & McEwin, C. K. (1994). *Growing pains: The making of America's middle school teachers*. Columbus, OH: National Middle School Association and Carrboro, NC: Center for Early Adolescence.

Seefeldt, V., & Branta, C. F. (1984). Patterns of participation in childrens' sports. In J. R. Thomas (Ed.), *Motor development during childhood and adolescence* (pp. 190-211). Minneapolis, MN: Burgess.

Sullivan, J. A., & Grana, W. A. (1990). *The pediatric athlete*. Park Ridge, IL: American Academy of Orthopaedic Surgeons.

Valentine, J., Clark, D. C., Irvin, J. L., Keefe, J. W., & Melton, G. (1993). *Leadership in middle level education: A national survey of middle level leaders and schools* (2nd ed.). Reston, VA: National Association of Secondary School Principals.

Valentine, J., Clark, D. C., Nickerson, N. C., & Keefe, J. W. (1981). *The middle level principalship: A survey of middle level principals and programs*. Reston, VA: National Association of Secondary School Principals.

Valentine, J., & Mogar, D. C. (1992). Middle level certification: An encouraging evolution. *Middle School Journal, 24*(2), 36-43.

Part IV

APPENDICES

(NOTE: Tables on 7-9 schools do not include data on the 9th grade)

TABLE A1
MEANS OF ARTICULATION

Means of Articulation	Percent				
	5-8	6-8	7-8	7-9	All
Joint Workshops With Teachers in Lower and/or Higher Grades	74	65	70	55	66
Joint Curriculum Planning Activities With Teachers of Lower and/or Higher Grades	71	64	65	59	64
Middle School Teacher Visitation of Elementary and/or High School	42	44	42	39	43
Giving Program Information to Elementary and/or High School	74	80	81	83	80
Obtaining or Providing Data Regarding the Students Leaving or Entering Your School	86	84	79	80	83
Student Visitation of the High School(s) for Orientation	79	78	70	64	75
Visitation of Your School by Students from Feeder Schools	84	90	85	89	88
Middle School Student Visits to Feeder Schools to Acquaint Elementary Students With Your Programs and Activities	40	51	50	51	50
Visitation of Your School by High School Representatives for the Purpose of Orientation	69	77	76	78	76

TABLE A2
DATES OF ESTABLISHMENT OF MIDDLE LEVEL SCHOOLS

Grade Organization	Percent					
	Before 1955	1955-62	1963-71	1972-79	1980-87	1988-92
5-8	4	4	17	32	28	16
6-8	4	4	12	21	30	29
7-8	13	9	17	16	21	24
7-9	20	17	26	12	9	17
All	7	6	15	20	26	25

TABLE A3
PERSONS DETERMINING GRADE ORGANIZATION
IN SCHOOLS ESTABLISHED AFTER 1987

Persons and Groups Involved	Percent				
	5-8	6-8	7-8	7-9	All
Principal(s)	83	63	88	41	69
Teachers	63	50	67	41	54
System-level Administrators	97	92	100	81	91
Accreditation Bodies	10	5	4	4	5
State Departments of Education	17	12	10	7	12
Outside Agency	13	6	2	0	6
Parents	30	39	41	30	38
Others	30	18	22	22	20

TABLE A4
MIDDLE LEVEL SCHOOLS USING CERTAIN PREPARATORY
ACTIVITIES PRIOR TO ORIGINAL OPENING

Activity	Percent				
	5-8	6-8	7-8	7-9	All
Year or More Faculty Study and District Planning	70	54	68	44	57
Year or More Study by Faculty Representatives at College or University	13	8	1	4	7
Representation in Specially Funded Planning Project	33	23	24	15	24
Summer Faculty Workshop Prior to School Opening	43	40	45	44	42
Occasional Planning Sessions of Prospective School Faculty Members	73	71	79	67	73
Visitation of School With Similar Plans Operating	87	78	90	85	82
Inservice Meetings of Prospective Faculty Members With Consultants	78	67	69	63	68

TABLE B1
LANGUAGE ARTS ORGANIZATIONAL PLANS

Grade Organization	Percent											
	Grade 5			Grade 6			Grade 7			Grade 8		
	IT	D	SC	IT	D	SC	IT	D	SC	IT	D	SC
Grades 5-8	46	20	34	53	29	18	36	63	1	31	69	1
Grades 6-8	--	--	--	59	29	11	53	43	4	45	50	5
Grades 7-8	--	--	--	--	--	--	47	45	8	44	49	7
Grades 7-9	--	--	--	--	--	--	42	49	9	29	61	10
All	46	20	34	58	29	12	49	46	6	42	53	5

IT: Interdisciplinary Teams
D: Departmentalization
SC: Self-Contained Classroom

TABLE B2
MATHEMATICS ORGANIZATIONAL PLANS

Grade Organization	Percent											
	Grade 5			Grade 6			Grade 7			Grade 8		
	IT	D	SC	IT	D	SC	IT	D	SC	IT	D	SC
Grades 5-8	44	23	33	52	31	17	34	66	1	31	69	1
Grades 6-8	--	--	--	58	32	11	49	46	5	42	53	5
Grades 7-8	--	--	--	--	--	--	43	48	8	40	52	7
Grades 7-9	--	--	--	--	--	--	37	54	9	25	65	9
All	44	23	33	57	32	11	45	49	5	39	56	5

IT: Interdisciplinary Teams
D: Departmentalization
SC: Self-Contained Classroom

TABLE B3
SOCIAL STUDIES ORGANIZATIONAL PLANS

Grade Organization	Percent											
	Grade 5			Grade 6			Grade 7			Grade 8		
	IT	D	SC	IT	D	SC	IT	D	SC	IT	D	SC
Grades 5-8	47	20	33	53	30	17	33	66	1	30	68	1
Grades 6-8	--	--	--	59	31	11	58	38	4	45	51	4
Grades 7-8	--	--	--	--	--	--	46	46	8	38	54	8
Grades 7-9	--	--	--	--	--	--	37	54	9	40	51	9
All	47	20	33	58	30	12	44	50	6	42	54	5

IT: Interdisciplinary Teams
D: Departmentalization
SC: Self-Contained Classroom

TABLE B4
SCIENCE ORGANIZATIONAL PLANS

Grade Organization	Percent											
	Grade 5			Grade 6			Grade 7			Grade 8		
	IT	D	SC	IT	D	SC	IT	D	SC	IT	D	SC
Grades 5-8	48	22	30	53	32	15	34	65	1	30	69	1
Grades 6-8	--	--	--	58	32	10	49	46	4	44	52	4
Grades 7-8	--	--	--	--	--	--	44	49	7	41	53	7
Grades 7-9	--	--	--	--	--	--	36	55	9	25	66	9
All	48	22	30	57	32	11	45	50	5	39	50	5

IT: Interdisciplinary Teams
D: Departmentalization
SC: Self-Contained Classroom

TABLE B5
ORGANIZATIONAL PLANS FOR HEALTH INSTRUCTION
GRADES 5-8 SCHOOLS

Instructional Plans	Percent			
	Grade 5	Grade 6	Grade 7	Grade 8
Separate Subject	39	39	44	44
With P. E.	7	8	13	16
With Science	49	48	36	34
Other	5	5	6	6

TABLE B6
ORGANIZATIONAL PLANS FOR
HEALTH INSTRUCTION
GRADES 7-8 SCHOOLS

Instructional Plans	Percent	
	Grade 7	Grade 8
Separate Subject	34	35
With P. E.	18	21
With Science	39	33
Other	9	11

TABLE B7
ORGANIZATIONAL PLANS FOR
HEALTH INSTRUCTION
GRADES 7-9 SCHOOLS

Instructional Plans	Percent	
	Grade 7	Grade 8
Separate Subject	37	43
With P. E.	25	28
With Science	32	23
Other	6	6

TABLE B8
ORGANIZATIONAL PLANS FOR HEALTH INSTRUCTION
ALL SCHOOLS

Instructional Plans	Percent			
	Grade 5	Grade 6	Grade 7	Grade 8
Separate Subject	39	34	40	40
With P. E.	7	10	16	19
With Science	49	50	37	33
Other	5	6	7	7

TABLE B9
ORGANIZATIONAL PLANS FOR READING INSTRUCTION
GRADES 5-8 SCHOOLS

Instructional Plans	Percent			
	Grade 5	Grade 6	Grade 7	Grade 8
Separate With Own Period	70	70	52	52
Separate, But Blocked With Another Content Area	20	22	15	11
Integrated With Another Content Area	12	14	28	30
Integrated Throughout the Total School Program	10	10	14	14
Other	3	3	4	4

TABLE B10
ORGANIZATIONAL PLANS FOR
READING INSTRUCTION
GRADES 7-8 SCHOOLS

Instructional Plans	Percent	
	Grade 7	Grade 8
Separate With Own Period	56	50
Separate, But Blocked With Another Content Area	9	8
Integrated With Another Content Area	35	36
Integrated Throughout the Total School Program	25	25
Other	2	9

TABLE B11
ORGANIZATIONAL PLANS FOR READING
INSTRUCTION
GRADES 7-9 SCHOOLS

Instructional Plans	Percent	
	Grade 7	Grade 8
Separate With Own Period	59	53
Separate, But Blocked With Another Content Area	5	5
Integrated With Another Content Area	33	35
Integrated Throughout the Total School Program	24	24
Other	4	5

TABLE B12
ORGANIZATIONAL PLANS FOR READING INSTRUCTION
ALL SCHOOLS

Instructional Plans	Percent			
	Grade 5	Grade 6	Grade 7	Grade 8
Separate With Own Period	70	62	51	46
Separate, But Blocked With Another Content Area	20	19	14	12
Integrated With Another Content Area	12	21	31	33
Integrated Throughout the Total School Program	10	13	14	20
Other	3	2	3	3

TABLE B13
SCHEDULING PLANS

Type of Scheduling	Grade	Percent of Schools				
		5-8	6-8	7-8	7-9	All
Self-Contained Classroom	5	30	--	--	--	30
	6	16	13	--	--	13
	7	2	8	13	2	9
	8	2	7	13	0	7
Daily Periods Uniform Length	5	49	--	--	--	49
	6	83	82	--	--	82
	7	83	84	90	88	86
	8	85	88	91	91	89
Flexible Scheduling	5	32	--	--	--	32
	6	36	40	--	--	39
	7	27	40	25	25	34
	8	23	27	23	20	25
Daily Periods Varying Length	5	8	--	--	--	8
	6	8	6	--	--	7
	7	5	5	4	4	5
	8	4	5	3	4	4

TABLE B14
RESPONDENTS INDICATING DAILY
PERIODS - VARYING LENGTH
GRADE SEVEN

Number of Periods	Percent				
	5-8	6-8	7-8	7-9	All
Five	1	2	3	2	2
Six	10	13	17	22	15
Seven	43	40	47	50	43
Eight	29	29	23	14	26

TABLE C1
BASIC SUBJECTS TAKEN ALL YEAR
BY ALL STUDENTS

Subjects	Percent				
	5-8	6-8	7-8	7-9	All
Language Arts	100	99	100	99	99
Mathematics	100	100	100	99	99
Science	98	95	91	81	93
Social Studies	99	97	98	92	97
Physical Education	83	75	75	64	75

TABLE C2
REQUIRED AND ELECTIVE SUBJECTS OFFERINGS
GRADES 5-8 SCHOOLS

Course	Percent			
	Grade 5	Grade 6	Grade 7	Grade 8
Agriculture Required	1	1	2	2
Elective	1	1	2	4
Art Required	74	73	59	50
Elective	7	12	35	35
Band Required	--	--	--	--
Elective	58	84	90	90
Careers Required	1	4	9	9
Elective	3	4	8	9
Chorus Required	--	--	--	--
Elective	14	46	68	69
Computers Required	46	50	52	48
Elective	10	13	23	31
Creative Writing Required	24	35	37	37
Elective	3	3	8	8
Foreign Language Required	11	15	17	18
Elective	6	7	18	27

Course	Percent			
	Grade 5	Grade 6	Grade 7	Grade 8
General Music Required	67	63	43	31
Elective	6	9	13	13
Health Required	67	71	74	69
Elective	1	1	4	4
Home Economics Required	21	26	43	34
Elective	5	7	21	31
Industrial Arts Required	18	29	36	33
Elective	3	22	22	32
Journalism Required	--	--	--	--
Elective	3	4	11	16
Orchestra Required	--	--	--	--
Elective	17	19	19	20
Reading Required	87	89	70	70
Elective	2	3	9	9
Sex Education Required	44	48	55	53
Elective	4	4	5	6
Speech Required	--	--	--	--
Elective	3	3	8	9
Typing Required	7	6	10	6
Elective	7	3	4	5

TABLE C3
REQUIRED AND ELECTIVE SUBJECTS
OFFERINGS
GRADES 7-8 SCHOOLS

Course	Percent	
	Grade 7	Grade 8
Agriculture Required	1	1
Elective	5	7
Art Required	42	30
Elective	49	60
Band Required	--	--
Elective	92	93
Careers Required	12	13
Elective	11	14
Chorus Required	--	--
Elective	76	79
Computers Required	38	32
Elective	29	40
Creative Writing Required	22	22
Elective	8	10
Foreign Language Required	12	13
Elective	42	55

Course	Percent	
	Grade 7	Grade 8
General Music Required	36	20
Elective	23	21
Health Required	64	57
Elective	7	9
Home Economics Required	33	23
Elective	41	53
Industrial Arts Required	31	27
Elective	39	53
Journalism Required	--	--
Elective	19	30
Orchestra Required	--	--
Elective	38	38
Reading Required	55	46
Elective	16	20
Sex Education Required	39	35
Elective	4	5
Speech Required	--	--
Elective	15	15
Typing Required	9	5
Elective	10	14

TABLE C4
REQUIRED AND ELECTIVE
SUBJECTS OFFERINGS
GRADES 7-9 SCHOOLS

Course	Percent	
	Grade 7	Grade 8
Agriculture Required	0	0
Elective	3	4
Art Required	43	23
Elective	44	51
Band Required	--	--
Elective	92	93
Careers Required	9	10
Elective	10	10
Chorus Required	--	--
Elective	77	85
Computers Required	24	20
Elective	28	42
Creative Writing Required	13	14
Elective	7	17
Foreign Language Required	13	10
Elective	34	60

Course	Percent	
	Grade 7	Grade 8
General Music Required	33	14
Elective	24	24
Health Required	50	51
Elective	7	7
Home Economics Required	34	22
Elective	43	63
Industrial Arts Required	33	22
Elective	7	27
Journalism Required	--	--
Elective	7	27
Orchestra Required	--	--
Elective	55	58
Reading Required	52	36
Elective	20	23
Sex Education Required	29	30
Elective	5	5
Speech Required	--	--
Elective	13	23
Typing Required	11	5
Elective	21	34

TABLE C5
REQUIRED AND ELECTIVE SUBJECTS OFFERINGS
ALL SCHOOLS

Course	Percent			
	Grade 5	Grade 6	Grade 7	Grade 8
Agriculture Required	1	1	1	1
Elective	1	1	3	5
Art Required	74	61	45	33
Elective	14	28	53	54
Band Required	--	--	--	--
Elective	58	90	93	93
Careers Required	1	8	12	15
Elective	3	8	11	15
Chorus Required	--	--	--	--
Elective	14	59	75	79
Computers Required	46	42	40	34
Elective	10	28	29	39
Creative Writing Required	24	27	25	24
Elective	3	4	8	10
Foreign Language Required	15	14	14	14
Elective	6	15	39	50

Course	Percent			
	Grade 5	Grade 6	Grade 7	Grade 8
General Music Required	67	48	32	21
Elective	6	21	22	21
Health Required	67	66	66	64
Elective	1	4	6	7
Home Economics Required	21	32	36	28
Elective	5	15	35	47
Industrial Arts Required	18	31	34	29
Elective	3	17	35	47
Journalism Required	--	--	--	--
Elective	3	6	17	27
Orchestra Required	--	--	--	--
Elective	17	33	38	38
Reading Required	87	82	61	52
Elective	2	3	12	14
Sex Education Required	44	43	41	42
Elective	4	4	5	6
Speech Required	--	--	--	--
Elective	3	6	13	15
Typing Required	7	8	8	10
Elective	7	5	11	15

TABLE C6
LENGTH OF TIME FOR SELECTED SEVENTH GRADE COURSES
GRADES 5-8 SCHOOLS

Courses	Percent		
	One Year	One-Half Year	Less Than One-Half Year
Band	92	6	2
Reading	90	7	3
Chorus	79	19	1
Orchestra	78	11	11
Creative Writing	68	11	21
Foreign Language	54	19	27
General Music	40	27	33
Health	29	23	48
Journalism	28	28	44
Computers	26	25	49
Art	23	31	46
Careers	22	27	52
Speech	19	27	54
Typing	19	31	50
Sex Education	16	9	75
Industrial Arts	15	32	53
Home Economics	13	31	56
Agriculture	0	22	78

TABLE C7
LENGTH OF TIME FOR SELECTED SEVENTH GRADE COURSES
GRADES 7-8 SCHOOLS

Courses	Percent		
	Year	One-Half Year	Less Than One-Half Year
Band	91	7	2
Orchestra	88	8	3
Reading	78	14	8
Chorus	77	17	7
Foreign Language	53	23	24
Creative Writing	51	18	31
Journalism	51	22	27
General Music	21	31	49
Speech	18	39	43
Art	15	37	48
Computers	13	35	53
Industrial Arts	13	37	51
Health	12	36	52
Home Economics	12	36	53
Typing	11	32	57
Agriculture	9	35	57
Careers	9	34	57
Sex Education	6	14	80

TABLE C8
LENGTH OF TIME FOR SELECTED SEVENTH GRADE COURSES
GRADES 7-9 SCHOOLS

Courses	Percent		
	Year	One-Half Year	Less Than One-Half Year
Band	91	7	2
Orchestra	87	9	4
Reading	74	21	6
Chorus	69	25	7
Foreign Language	60	18	22
Agriculture	50	25	25
Journalism	45	45	9
Creative Writing	43	30	27
Art	32	11	57
Careers	30	28	43
General Music	29	32	39
Speech	25	39	36
Typing	21	46	32
Industrial Arts	20	42	38
Health	19	36	45
Home Economics	17	43	40
Computers	16	35	49
Sex Education	15	21	64

TABLE C9
LENGTH OF TIME FOR SELECTED SEVENTH GRADE COURSES
ALL SCHOOLS

Courses	Percent		
	Year	One-Half Year	Less Than One-Half Year
Band	90	7	2
Orchestra	86	10	4
Reading	83	11	6
Chorus	74	18	7
Creative Writing	57	16	27
Foreign Language	48	23	28
Journalism	42	28	30
General Music	26	29	45
Speech	25	32	43
Health	20	31	50
Art	18	32	50
Computers	16	32	52
Careers	15	29	57
Industrial Arts	15	35	50
Typing	15	36	48
Agriculture	11	32	57
Home Economics	11	36	53
Sex Education	10	12	78

TABLE C10
SELECTED STUDENT ACTIVITIES
GRADES 5-8 SCHOOLS

Activity	Percent			
	Grade 5	Grade 6	Grade 7	Grade 8
Honor Society	11	15	30	34
Publications	24	29	44	52
Student Council	72	76	83	85
Social Dancing	24	34	67	68
School Parties	72	74	63	63

TABLE C11
SELECTED STUDENT ACTIVITIES
GRADES 7-8 SCHOOLS

Activity	Percent	
	Grade 7	Grade 8
Honor Society	46	56
Publications	50	64
Student Council	92	94
Social Dancing	67	68
School Parties	71	72

TABLE C12
SELECTED STUDENT ACTIVITIES
GRADES 7-9 SCHOOLS

Activity	Percent	
	Grade 7	Grade 8
Honor Society	36	63
Publications	40	57
Student Council	90	91
Social Dancing	65	65
School Parties	61	61

TABLE C13
SELECTED STUDENT ACTIVITIES
ALL SCHOOLS

Activity	Percent			
	Grade 5	Grade 6	Grade 7	Grade 8
Honor Society	11	19	41	48
Publications	24	35	61	61
Student Council	72	83	87	90
Social Dancing	24	53	67	67
School Parties	72	70	67	68

TABLE D1
USE OF SELECTED INSTRUCTIONAL STRATEGIES
GRADES 5-8 SCHOOLS

Strategy	Percent of Use											
	Rarely				Occasionally				Regularly			
	5	6	7	8	5	6	7	8	5	6	7	8
Direct Instruction	2	2	1	1	12	10	9	9	86	88	91	91
Cooperative Learning	3	3	5	5	46	46	49	49	51	51	46	45
Inquiry-Teaching	13	10	12	11	59	46	49	49	28	28	28	29
Independent Study	39	36	34	34	48	50	51	50	13	14	16	16

TABLE D2
USE OF SELECTED INSTRUCTIONAL STRATEGIES
GRADES 7-8 SCHOOLS

Strategy	Percent of Use					
	Rarely		Occas.		Reg.	
	7	8	7	8	7	8
Direct Instruction	1	1	8	8	91	92
Cooperative Learning	4	4	48	48	49	48
Inquiry-Teaching	10	10	56	56	34	33
Independent Study	28	28	54	54	18	18

Occas.: Occasionally
Reg.: Regularly

TABLE D3
USE OF SELECTED INSTRUCTIONAL STRATEGIES
GRADES 7-9 SCHOOLS

Strategy	Percent of Use					
	Rarely		Occas.		Reg.	
	7	8	7	8	7	8
Direct Instruction	1	1	4	4	95	95
Cooperative Learning	3	3	50	51	47	46
Inquiry-Teaching	10	10	49	52	41	39
Independent Study	29	30	38	37	33	34

Occas.: Occasionally
Reg.: Regularly

TABLE D4
USE OF SELECTED INSTRUCTIONAL STRATEGIES
ALL SCHOOLS

Strategy	Percent of Use											
	Rarely				Occasionally				Regularly			
	5	6	7	8	5	6	7	8	5	6	7	8
Direct Instruction	2	1	1	1	12	10	9	8	86	88	90	91
Cooperative Learning	3	3	3	4	46	43	47	48	51	54	50	48
Inquiry-Teaching	13	9	10	10	59	56	56	56	28	34	35	34
Independent Study	39	31	29	29	48	51	51	51	13	18	20	20

TABLE D5
INDEPENDENT STUDY OPPORTUNITIES
GRADES 5-8 SCHOOLS

Type of Independent Study	Percent			
	Grade 5	Grade 6	Grade 7	Grade 8
Some students are released part or all of the time from the class(es) for independent study	25	25	27	27
One or more groups of students with similar interests work as a seminar	14	15	18	20
Some students have individual planned programs with regular scheduled time for independent study	16	17	21	21
Some students have time scheduled for work experience with faculty supervision	5	6	8	13

TABLE D6
INDEPENDENT STUDY OPPORTUNITIES
GRADES 6-8 SCHOOLS

Type of Independent Study	Percent		
	Grade 6	Grade 7	Grade 8
Some students are released part or all of the time from the class(es) for independent study	22	23	26
One or more groups of students with similar interests work as a seminar	15	16	18
Some students have individual planned programs with regular scheduled time for independent study	14	16	18
Some students have time scheduled for work experience with faculty supervision	8	11	15

TABLE D7
INDEPENDENT STUDY OPPORTUNITIES
GRADES 7-8 SCHOOLS

Type of Independent Study	Percent	
	Grade 7	Grade 8
Some students are released part or all of the time from the class(es) for independent study	22	27
One or more groups of students with similar interests work as a seminar	15	14
Some students have individual planned programs with regular scheduled time for independent study	17	19
Some students have time scheduled for work experience with faculty supervision	11	15

TABLE D8
INDEPENDENT STUDY OPPORTUNITIES
GRADES 7-9 SCHOOLS

Type of Independent Study	Percent	
	Grade 7	Grade 8
Some students are released part or all of the time from the class(es) for independent study	16	21
One or more groups of students with similar interests work as a seminar	11	10
Some students have individual planned programs with regular scheduled time for independent study	16	17
Some students have time scheduled for work experience with faculty supervision	9	15

TABLE D9
INDEPENDENT STUDY OPPORTUNITIES
ALL SCHOOLS

Type of Independent Study	Percent			
	Grade 5	Grade 6	Grade 7	Grade 8
Some students are released part or all of the time from the class(es) for independent study	25	22	22	26
One or more groups of students with similar interests work as a seminar	14	15	23	17
Some students have individually planned programs with regular scheduled time for independent study	16	15	24	18
Some students have time scheduled for work experience with faculty supervision	5	8	15	15

TABLE D10
PUPIL PROGRESS REPORTING

Types of Progress Reports	Percent				
	5-8	6-8	7-8	7-9	All
Letter Scale	83	80	82	86	81
Word Scale	31	20	13	20	19
Number Scale	12	10	9	10	10
Satisfactory-Unsatisfactory	44	38	34	29	37
Informal Written Notes	64	60	56	52	58
Percentage Marks	35	32	29	31	32
Portfolio	20	22	22	16	21
Parent Conferences	74	62	58	54	61

TABLE E1
CRITERIA EMPLOYED IN STUDENT ASSIGNMENT
GRADES 5-8 SCHOOLS

Criteria	Percent of Type of Grouping											
	Homebase Advisory Group				Required Content Subjects				Elective Content Subjects			
	5	6	7	8	5	6	7	8	5	6	7	8
I. Q. Tests	1	1	1	1	10	11	12	12	2	2	4	4
Achievement Tests	7	6	5	5	33	34	35	38	5	5	9	11
Teacher Recommend-ations	23	22	19	19	54	56	57	58	11	12	19	21
Parental Input	12	12	11	11	10	9	11	10	14	17	22	23
Previous Academic Record	8	8	7	7	42	46	47	50	23	26	37	36
Random Assignment	42	44	46	46	48	49	51	51	46	47	49	49

TABLE E2
CRITERIA EMPLOYED IN STUDENT ASSIGNMENT
GRADES 7-8 SCHOOLS

Criteria	Percent of Type of Grouping					
	H.B.A.		R.C.S.		E.C.S.	
	7	8	7	8	7	8
I. Q. Tests	1	1	17	17	5	5
Achievement Tests	3	3	52	52	10	11
Teacher Recommend-ations	7	6	63	63	25	28
Parental Input	4	3	10	10	33	33
Previous Academic Record	4	4	57	57	34	34
Random Assignment	43	43	55	55	58	59

H.B.A: Homebase Advisory Groups
R.C.S.: Required Content Subjects
E.C.S.: Elective Content Subjects

TABLE E3
CRITERIA EMPLOYED IN STUDENT ASSIGNMENT
GRADES 7-9 SCHOOLS

Criteria	Percent of Type of Grouping					
	H.B.A.		R.C.S.		E.C.S.	
	7	8	7	8	7	8
I. Q. Tests	1	1	17	17	5	5
AchievementTests	4	4	51	53	11	10
Teacher Recommendations	5	5	67	68	32	34
Parental Input	4	4	9	9	36	38
Previous Academic Record	4	4	61	65	32	34
Random Assignment	32	32	39	39	51	49

H.B.A: Homebase Advisory Groups
R.C.S.: Required Content Subjects
E.C.S.: Elective Content Subjects

TABLE E4
CRITERIA EMPLOYED IN STUDENT ASSIGNMENT
ALL SCHOOLS

Criteria	Percent of Type of Grouping											
	Homebase Advisory Group				Required Content Subjects				Elective Content Subjects			
	5	6	7	8	5	6	7	8	5	6	7	8
I. Q. Tests	1	1	1	1	10	10	16	16	2	1	3	4
Achievement Tests	7	3	4	4	33	29	48	48	5	4	9	10
Teacher Recommend-ations	23	10	12	11	54	58	61	62	11	11	23	25
Parental Input	12	5	6	6	10	6	9	9	14	14	27	28
Previous Academic Record	8	4	5	5	42	34	44	56	23	20	32	33
Random Assignment	42	33	45	45	48	35	51	51	46	36	55	55

TABLE F1
SCHOOLS ENGAGING IN PLANNING AND
STAFF DEVELOPMENT PRIOR TO
IMPLEMENTING TEACHER-BASED
GUIDANCE PROGRAMS

Grade Organization	Number	Percent
5-8	79	78
6-8	446	83
7-8	139	81
7-9	45	79
All	709	82

TABLE F2
SCHOOLS WHERE ALL PROFESSIONAL
STAFF SERVE AS ADVISORS

Grade Organization	Number	Percent
5-8	51	53
6-8	320	59
7-8	94	54
7-9	27	46
All	492	56

TABLE F3
STAFF OTHER THAN CLASSROOM TEACHERS WHO SERVE AS ADVISORS

Position	Percent				
	5-8	6-8	7-8	7-9	All
Administrators	41	25	24	29	27
Media Specialists	48	37	31	29	36
Resource Teachers	70	57	49	53	56
Counselors	61	37	34	51	39
Other	10	6	7	14	7

TABLE G1
INTRAMURAL AND INTERSCHOLASTIC SPORTS
GRADES 5-8 SCHOOLS

Activity	Percent			
	Grade 5	Grade 6	Grade 7	Grade 8
Intramural Sports (Boys)	55	55	48	48
Intramural Sports (Girls)	55	55	48	48
Interscholastic Sports (Boys)	12	19	79	82
Interscholastic Sports (Girls)	12	19	78	81

TABLE G2
INTRAMURAL AND INTERSCHOLASTIC SPORTS
GRADES 7-8 SCHOOLS

Activity	Percent	
	Grade 7	Grade 8
Intramural Sports (Boys)	62	61
Intramural Sports (Girls)	62	61
Interscholastic Sports (Boys)	80	81
Interscholastic Sports (Girls)	79	81

TABLE G3
INTRAMURAL AND INTERSCHOLASTIC SPORTS
GRADES 7-9 SCHOOLS

Activity	Percent	
	Grade 7	Grade 8
Intramural Sports (Boys)	58	58
Intramural Sports (Girls)	58	58
Interscholastic Sports (Boys)	70	78
Interscholastic Sports (Girls)	70	77

TABLE G4
INTRAMURAL AND INTERSCHOLASTIC SPORTS
ALL SCHOOLS

Activity	Percent			
	Grade 5	Grade 6	Grade 7	Grade 8
Intramural Sports (Boys)	54	62	58	57
Intramural Sports (Girls)	55	61	58	57
Interscholastic Sports (Boys)	12	25	77	80
Interscholastic Sports (Girls)	12	25	76	79

TABLE G5
INTERSCHOLASTIC SPORTS PROGRAMS
GRADES 5-8 SCHOOLS

Interscholastic Sports	Percent							
	Grade 5		Grade 6		Grade 7		Grade 8	
	B	G	B	G	B	G	B	G
Football	3	1	6	1	55	6	59	6
Basketball	13	12	21	21	85	84	88	87
Baseball	3	1	8	1	24	4	26	4
Softball	3	6	4	10	5	30	5	31
Track	8	8	14	14	65	65	67	67
Wrestling	6	1	8	1	39	6	41	6
Swimming	4	4	5	5	8	9	9	9
Gymnastics	0	2	0	2	1	5	1	5
Tennis	1	1	1	1	10	11	11	11
Volleyball	2	5	3	7	7	47	7	51
Soccer	5	5	9	9	20	18	21	18
Cross Country	4	4	6	6	27	27	28	28

B: Boys
G: Girls

TABLE G6
INTERSCHOLASTIC SPORTS
GRADES 7-8 SCHOOLS

Interscholastic Sports	Percent			
	Grade 7		Grade 8	
	B	G	B	G
Football	56	9	61	9
Basketball	83	82	87	86
Baseball	23	3	24	4
Softball	8	31	8	33
Track	73	73	75	75
Wrestling	43	5	45	5
Swimming	9	10	9	10
Gymnastics	2	7	2	8
Tennis	12	12	13	13
Volleyball	13	63	15	65
Soccer	23	22	24	22
Cross Country	36	35	37	36

B: Boys
G: Girls

TABLE G7
INTERSCHOLASTIC SPORTS
GRADES 7-9 SCHOOLS

Interscholastic Sports	Percent			
	Grade 7		Grade 8	
	B	G	B	G
Football	60	4	72	7
Basketball	77	76	84	83
Baseball	29	4	34	5
Softball	7	35	8	41
Track	69	69	75	75
Wrestling	51	2	88	4
Swimming	14	16	16	17
Gymnastics	7	16	7	17
Tennis	23	27	25	30
Volleyball	10	56	11	58
Soccer	25	22	27	25
Cross Country	30	28	34	33

B: Boys
G: Girls

TABLE G8
INTERSCHOLASTIC SPORTS PROGRAMS
ALL SCHOOLS

Interscholastic Sports	Percent							
	Grade 5		Grade 6		Grade 7		Grade 8	
	B	G	B	G	B	G	B	G
Football	3	1	8	1	56	6	62	7
Basketball	13	12	24	24	82	81	86	84
Baseball	3	1	7	1	22	3	24	3
Softball	3	6	5	11	7	29	7	32
Track	8	8	23	23	70	70	72	72
Wrestling	6	1	11	2	41	2	43	5
Swimming	4	4	4	4	9	9	9	10
Gymnastics	0	2	2	3	3	7	3	17
Tennis	1	1	4	4	15	15	16	16
Volleyball	2	5	7	15	11	57	12	59
Soccer	5	5	11	10	24	22	25	23
Cross Country	4	4	13	13	30	30	32	32

B: Boys
G: Girls

nmsa

NATIONAL MIDDLE SCHOOL ASSOCIATION
4807 Evanswood Drive
Columbus, Ohio 43229-6292
(614)848-8211   FAX (614)848-4301

MIDDLE LEVEL SCHOOL SURVEY
1·9·9·2

This survey is being conducted as a follow up of William M. Alexander's pioneer 1967 survey and one he conducted with C. Kenneth McEwin in 1987. The purpose is to find out more about the progress, both numerically and programmatically, of middle level schools since these earlier surveys.

Your school has been selected in a nation wide sample of middle level schools. We realize that your time is valuable and limited, but also understand that middle level education is currently undergoing rapid changes that may not be reflected in earlier studies. Your cooperation in completing this form promptly will be greatly appreciated, and you will be sent a copy of the survey report if requested.

C. Kenneth McEwin
Professor
Appalachian State University

Doris M. Jenkins
Associate Professor
Appalachian State University

Thomas S. Dickinson
Editor, *Middle School Journal*
National Middle School Association

GENERAL INFORMATION

1. Name _____   Title _____

2. Name of School _____   Current Enrollment_____

3. School Address _____

    City _____   State _____   Zip _____

4. *Do you wish to be sent a copy of the report of this survey?*

    ☐ *Yes*   ☐ *No*

ADMINISTRATIVE ORGANIZATION

5. Please indicate by a check (✔) the grades included in your school:

    ☐ 5-8   ☐ 6-8   ☐ 7-8   ☐ 7-9   ☐ Other _____

ARTICULATION

6. Please indicate by a check (✔) any of the following means employed by your school to provide articulation between your school and those with lower and/or higher grades:

    ☐ Joint workshops with teachers in lower and/or higher grades

    ☐ Joint curriculum planning activities with teachers of lower and/or higher grades

    ☐ Middle school teacher visitation of elementary and/or high schools

    ☐ Giving program information to elementary and/or high schools

    ☐ Obtaining or providing data regarding students entering or leaving your school

    ☐ Student visitation of the high school(s) for orientation

    ☐ Visitation of your school by students from feeder schools

    ☐ Middle school students' visits to feeder schools to acquaint elementary students with your program and facilities

    ☐ Visitation of your school by high school representatives for the purpose of orientation

    ☐ Other (specify) _____

ESTABLISHMENT OF YOUR SCHOOL

7. Please indicate by a check (✔) the year your middle level school was established:

☐ Before 1955   ☐ 1955-62   ☐ 1963-71   ☐ 1972-79   ☐ 1980-87   ☐ 1988-1992

If your school was established in 1988 or later, please respond to numbers 8 and 9.

If it was established before 1988, please skip these questions and move to number 10.

8. Please indicate by as many checks (✔s) as applicable the person(s) involved in deciding on your grade organization:

☐ Principal(s)   ☐ State department of education

☐ Teachers   ☐ Survey by an outside agency

☐ System-level administration   ☐ Parents

☐ Accrediting bodies   ☐ Other (specify) _____

9. Please indicate by as many checks (✔s) as applicable the activities in which your staff participated prior to opening your present middle level school:

☐ A year or more of full-time faculty study and planning, in your district

☐ A year or more of full-time study by faculty representatives at a college or university in a program designed specifically to prepare middle level teachers

☐ Representation in a specially funded middle school planning project

☐ Summer faculty workshop prior to the opening of the school year

☐ Occasional planning sessions of prospective middle school faculty members

☐ Visitation of schools with similar plans in operation, by representatives of your school

☐ Inservice meetings of prospective faculty members with consultant(s) on middle level school development

☐ Other (Please specify) _____

_____

_____

_____

CURRICULUM

10. Please indicate by as many checks (✓s) as applicable whether each of these subjects is taken by all students in all grades (all year) and explain the situation for each "No":

Subject	Check		Explanation, if "No"
	Yes	No	
Language Arts			
Mathematics			
Physical Education			
Science			
Social Studies			

11. Please indicate by grades, any subject(s) in which opportunities are provided for some students to work independently of a class:

Type of Independent Study	Write in, by grades, any subject(s) in which used				
	5	6	7	8	9
Some students are released part or all of the time from the class(es) for independent study					
One or more groups of students with similiar interests work as a seminar					
Some students have individually-planned programs with regularly scheduled time for independent study					
Some students have time scheduled for work experience with faculty supervision					

12. Please place a check (✓) in each box to indicate required and elective courses at each grade level:

Course	Required Courses						Elective Courses					
	All	5	6	7	8	9	All	5	6	7	8	9
Agriculture												
Art												
Band												
Careers												
Chorus												
Computers												
Creative Writing												
Foreign Language												
General Music												
Health												
Home Economics												
Industrial Arts												
Journalism												
Orchestra												
Reading												
Sex Education												
Speech												
Typing												
Others: *												

* If your list includes too many "others" to list here, please enclose a copy with information noted as to grades as above.

13. Please place a check (✔) as applicable to indicate length of courses offered at the **seventh grade level:**

Seventh Grade Courses	Year	1/2 Year	Less than 1/2 Year
Agriculture			
Art			
Band			
Careers			
Chorus			
Computers			
Creative Writing			
Foreign Language			
General Music			
Health			
Home Economics			
Industrial Arts			
Journalism			
Orchestra			
Reading			
Sex Education			
Speech			
Typing			
Others: *			

* If your list includes too many "others" to list here, please enclose a copy with information noted as above.

14. Please indicate by as many checks (✓s) as applicable in what grades each of the following is offered, if at all:

Activity	Grades					
	All	5	6	7	8	9
Intramural Sports (Boys)						
Intramural Sports (Girls)						
Interscholastic Sports (Boys)						
Interscholastic Sports (Girls)						
Honor Society						
Publications						
Student Council						
Social Dancing						
School Parties						
Others:*						

* If your list includes too many "others" to list here, please enclose a copy with information noted as above.

15. Does your school have an interest class/mini-course program (short-term, student interest-centered courses)?

☐ Yes   ☐ No

If yes, most courses meet for _____ weeks, _____ days per week.

Comments: _____

_____

_____

_____

INSTRUCTION

16. Please write in the grade(s) in which each instructional plan is followed for the subjects listed. Just write "all" if there are no differences among grade levels in your school:

Instructional Plan	In what grade(s) is each instructional plan followed for each subject?			
	Language Arts	Math	Social Studies	Science
Interdisciplinary Team - 2 or more teachers working together with same students in 2 or more of these subjects)				
Departmental- (different class and teacher for each subject)				
Self-contained Classroom- (one teacher for all the basic subjects)				
Other plan- Explain: _____ _____				

Comments: _____

_____

17. If your school utilizes interdisciplinary teams of teachers, how are team leaders selected? Please check (✔) one:

☐ No team leader is identified

☐ Appointed by principal or other school official

☐ Elected by other members of teaching team

☐ Leader rotates among members over time

☐ Leader emerges informally as the team works together

☐ Other _____

18. Please indicate by a check (✓) the approximate percentage of interdisciplinary instruction (specifically designed units of instruction) ongoing in your school.

   ☐   1 - 20%

   ☐   21 - 40%

   ☐   41 - 60%

   ☐   61 - 80%

   ☐   81 -100%

19. Please indicate by a check (✓) how health is taught in your school at each grade level:

Health	Grades					
	All	5	6	7	8	9
Separate Subject						
With Physical Education						
With Science						
Other:						

20. Please indicate by a check (✓) how reading is taught in your school at each grade level:

Reading	Grades					
	All	5	6	7	8	9
Separate subject with its own period						
Separate subject, but blocked with another content area						
Integrated with another content area						
Integrated throughout the total school program						
Other*						

*If your list includes too many "others" to list here, please enclose a copy with information noted as above.

21. Please check (✓) the statement which best describes the status of planning periods for teachers at your school.

   ☐   All have one planning period (not including lunch).

   ☐   All teachers have two planning periods (not including lunch).

   ☐   Most teachers have one planning period (not including lunch).

   ☐   Most teachers have two planning periods (not including lunch).

   ☐   Teachers do not have a planning period (not including lunch).

22. Please check (✓) the extent to which the following teaching methods or strategies are used in your school:

Strategy	Extent of Use by Grade Level											
	Rarely or Never				Occasionally (A few times each month)				Regularly (Every week)			
	5	6	7	8	5	6	7	8	5	6	7	8
Direct Instruction- (teacher presentation drill, practice, etc.)												
Cooperative Learning- (structured group work and rewards for achievement)												
Inquiry Teaching- (gathering information, deriving conclusions)												
Independent Study- (working individually on selected or assigned tasks)												

23. Please indicate by as many checks (✓s) as applicable the criteria employed in assigning students to various types of classroom groups at each grade level:

Criteria	Type of Grouping											
	Homebase Advisory Groups				Required Content Subjects				Elective Content Subjects			
Grades	5	6	7	8	5	6	7	8	5	6	7	8
I.Q. Tests												
Acheivement Tests												
Teacher Recommendations												
Parental Input												
Previous Academic Record												
Random Assignment												

24. Please check (✓) the statement below that best describes your school's operating policy toward "ability" grouping (homogeneous vs. heterogenous) of students for instruction? If your school does not ability group, check (✓) "Grouping is random."

☐ Grouping is carried out at all grade levels in all subject areas.

☐ Grouping is carried out at all grade levels, but restricted to certain subject areas.

☐ Grouping is carried out only at certain grades levels, but the grouping is done in all subject areas at those levels.

☐ Grouping is carried out only at certain grade levels, and is restricted to certain subject areas at those grade levels.

☐ We have a grouping system different from the alternatives above.
   Describe: _____

_____

_____

_____

☐ Grouping is random.

25. Please indicate remedial arrangements available to students at your school. Check (✓) all that apply:

☐ No special programs, it is up to the students to stay on grade level

☐ Extra work or homework by classroom teacher

☐ Pull-out program in English/Language arts

☐ Pull-out program in mathematics

☐ Extra subject period instead of elective or exploratory course

☐ After-school or before-school classes or coaching sessions

☐ Saturday Classes

☐ Summer school

☐ Other (Describe) _____

26. In your opinion, what approximate percent of time does a typical student in your school spend in each of the following instructional groupings?

Groupings	Example	Grades			
		5	6	7	8
Large Group Instruction (More than 25)	5%				
Traditional Class Size (20 to 25)	80%				
Small Group Instruction (2 to 15)	10%				
Individualized Instruction	5%				
Totals	100%	100%	100%	100%	100%

27. Please indicate by as many checks (✔s) as applicable the type(s) of daily scheduling utilized in your school at each grade level:

Type of Schedule		Grades			
		5	6	7	8
Self-contained classrooms					
Daily periods uniform in length (Not including lunch)	5 Period Day				
	6 Period Day				
	7 Period Day				
	8 Period Day				
Flexible scheduling within blocks for teams					
Daily periods of varying length (explain)					
Other plan (explain)					

Comments: _____

_____

_____

_____

28. Please indicate by as many checks (✔s) as applicable the system(s) your school uses for reporting pupil progress to parents:

- ☐ Letter scale (A to F, etc.)
- ☐ Word scale (Excellent, good, etc.)
- ☐ Number scale (1-5, etc.)
- ☐ Satisfactory-Unsatisfactory scale (S, U; Pass-Fail, Etc.)
- ☐ Informal written notes
- ☐ Percentage marks (90, 80, etc.)
- ☐ Portfolio
- ☐ Regularly-scheduled parent conferences
- ☐ Other (specify) _____

29. Do you have a teacher-based guidance program (advisor/advisee, homebase) in your school?

    ☐ Yes   ☐ No

    If yes, please answer questions 30-34. If no, please move to question 35.

30. Did your school engage in a planning process and offer staff development activities prior to implementing the program?

    ☐ Yes   ☐ No

31. Do all full-time professional staff serve as homebase teachers/advisors?

    ☐ Yes   ☐ No

32. Which, if any, staff members other than teachers are advisors? Please check (✔) your choices:

    ☐ Administrators

    ☐ Media Specialists

    ☐ Resource Teachers

    ☐ Counselors

    ☐ Other: (Please specify) _____

33. How often do your advisory groups meet? Please check (✔) your choice:

    ☐ Daily

    ☐ Four days per week

    ☐ Three days per week

    ☐ Two days per week

    ☐ Once a week

    ☐ Two times a month

    ☐ Other (Please specify) _____

34. How many minutes per session do the homebase/advisory groups meet? _____

FACULTY PREPARATION

35. Please check (✔) the approximate percentage of your faculty who have had specific university preparation for middle level teaching:

    ☐ Less than 25%   ☐ 25 to 50%   ☐ 51-75%   ☐ 76-100%

36. In your opinion, what percentage of teachers at your school are awaiting the opportunity to take a position at an elementary or senior-high school. Please check (✔) your choice:

   ☐ None

   ☐ 1 - 20%

   ☐ 21 - 40%

   ☐ 41 - 60%

   ☐ 61 - 80%

   ☐ 81 - 100%

SPORTS

37. Listed below are sports often played at the middle level. Please check (✔) the grade levels of interscholastic sports available at your school for boys and girls.

Interscholastic Sports	Grade 5		Grade 6		Grade 7		Grade 8	
	Boys	Girls	Boys	Girls	Boys	Girls	Boys	Girls
Football								
Basketball								
Baseball								
Softball								
Track								
Wrestling								
Swimming								
Gymnastics								
Tennis								
Volleyball								
Soccer								
Cross Country								
Other								

38. What changes, if any, have been made in your scholastic sports program in the last ten years? Check (✓) all that apply:

    ☐ Eliminated sport(s) (Please specify) _____

    ☐ Reduced number of games

    ☐ Play only schools in your school district

    ☐ Play only schools from adjacent school districts

    ☐ Play only schools within 50 miles of your school

    ☐ No change

    ☐ New sports added (Please specify) _____

    ☐ Other (Please specify) _____

ADDITIONAL INFORMATION

39. Please describe any plan you have for evaluating your school, enclosing any available illustrative materials: _____

_____

_____

40. Please list any major problems you have encountered in your move toward an effective middle level program: _____

_____

_____

41. What elements of your school do you consider exemplary?

_____

_____

_____

42. Other comments:

_____

_____

_____

_____

NATIONAL MIDDLE SCHOOL ASSOCIATION

National Middle School Association was established in 1973 to serve as a voice for professionals and others interested in the education of young adolescents. The Association has grown rapidly and now enrolls members in all fifty states, the Canadian provinces, and forty-two other nations. In addition, fifty-two state, regional, and provincial middle school associations are official affiliates of NMSA.

NMSA is the only association dedicated exclusively to the education, development, and growth of young adolescents. Membership is open to all. While middle level teachers and administrators make up the bulk of the membership, central office personnel, college and university faculty, state department officials, other professionals, parents, and lay citizens are also actively involved in supporting our single mission – improving the educational experiences of 10 -15 year olds. This open membership is a particular strength of NMSA.

The Association provides a variety of services, conferences, and materials in fulfilling its mission. In addition to the *Middle School Journal*, the movement's premier professional journal, the Association publishes the *Research in Middle Level Education Quarterly*, a wealth of books and monographs, videos, a general newsletter, an urban education newspaper, and occasional papers. The Association's highly acclaimed annual conference, which has drawn over 10,000 registrants in recent years, is held in the fall.

For information about NMSA and its many services contact the Headquarters at 2600 Corporate Exchange Drive, Suite 370, Columbus, Ohio 43231, TELEPHONE 800-528-NMSA, FAX 614-895-4750.

National Middle School Association
2600 Corporate Exchange Drive, Suite 370
Columbus, Ohio 43231

Executive Director
Sue Swaim

Director of Member and Affiliate Services
Jim Burns

Director of Professional Development
Lynn Wallich

Director of Business Services
Jeff Ward